LIFE AND DEATH IN PSYCHOANALYSIS

Life and Death in Psychoanalysis

Jean Laplanche

Published in France by Flammarion as
Vie et mort en psychanalyse

TRANSLATED

WITH AN INTRODUCTION BY

Jeffrey Mehlman

THE JOHNS HOPKINS UNIVERSITY PRESS

Baltimore and London

This book has been brought to publication with the generous assistance of the Andrew W. Mellon Foundation.

Originally published in 1970 as *Vie et mort en psychanalyse.*
Copyright © 1970, Flammarion

Copyright © 1976. The Johns Hopkins University Press
All rights reserved. Published 1976
Printed in the United States of America on acid-free paper

Johns Hopkins Paperbacks edition, 1985
06 05 04 03 02 01 00 99 98 97   8 7 6 5 4

The Johns Hopkins University Press
2715 North Charles Street
Baltimore, Maryland 21218-4319
The Johns Hopkins Press Ltd., London

Library of Congress Cataloging-in-Publication Data

Laplanche, Jean.
  Life and death in psychoanalysis.

  Translation of Vie et mort en psychanalyse.
  1. Freud, Sigmund, 1856–1939. 2. Psychoanalysis. 3. Conflict (Psychology)   I. Title.
[DNLM: 1. Psychoanalytic theory. WM460 L314v]
BF73.F85L2713   150´.19´52   75-36928
ISBN 0-8018-1637-8 (hardcover)
ISBN 0-8018-2730-2 (paperback)

A catalog record for this book is available from the British Library.

Contents

Translator's Introduction

In recent years, it has become increasingly—at times, disquietingly—clear that one of the rare and most intense sources of intellectual energy currently available to literate intellectuals has been a series of readings, performed in France, of certain German-language texts. Of those texts none has been read to more remarkable effect than that of Freud, and it is to one of the crucial readings in that general endeavor, Jean Laplanche's *Life and Death in Psychoanalysis*—to its situation in the recent "return to Freud" in France, to the way it functions, and to the role that it alone might play for an English-language readership—that these remarks are devoted.

It should be emphasized that this contribution to (and/or reversal of) psychoanalytic theory is above all an exemplary act of reading. In taking calculated risks with the text, in temporarily suspending the question of empirical reference in favor of considerations of structure, the French have pressed their wager with Freud to the point where the payoffs have been handsome indeed. Laplanche, in particular, has given us nothing less than a poetics of Freud's work. But the error here would be to assume that such a poetics is contingent upon or secondary to an understanding of the text, that the French are giving us nothing more than an updated brief for rewarding Freud the Goethe Prize for Literature. For the thrust of the French reading is that *until* we grasp the poetics of Freud's work, the general economy of that work—i.e., its ultimate import—will escape us. More specifically, Laplanche has demonstrated that unless we realize that several key "nodes" in Freud's thought are structured unwittingly according to the rhetorical figure of chiasmus, Freud's last theory of drives, in particular, can only be a source of bafflement.

There is a ruse in recent intellectual history which has resulted in the following paradox: the most powerful—i.e., both stunning and convincing—act of reading currently available to us (generically: the French re-reading of Freud) has been performed on a nonliterary work. This situation has been immensely inconvenient to the professionals of reading (. . . literature) in this country, and more especially (and more comically) so to that small and threatened clerisy charged with representing "French culture" in the universities. For it has done nothing less than drive a chink into the wall behind which, with undeniable subtlety, they pursue the somewhat tautological business of demonstrating the profound "literarity" of literature. I confess that in translating Laplanche, I hope to contribute to a widening of that chink.

Any consideration of the "return to Freud" in France must come to some terms with the work of Jacques Lacan. For it was within the (relative) secrecy of Lacan's (immense) seminar that many of the readings under consideration were spawned. In 1966, Lacan finally published the thousand pages of *Ecrits*, containing a dazzling assortment of superlatively provocative and outrageously intelligent observations born of his analyses of Freud. The crucial point in this context, however, is that those analyses themselves, for the most part, do not appear in *Ecrits*. There has thus been an unfortunate tendency in France for those observations to degenerate into polemical ploys or instruments of intimidation in the writings of Lacan's epigones. I would suggest, on the basis of personal experience, that the best entry into (French) Freud for an American would follow the quintessentially Freudian temporal scheme delineated by Laplanche in the second chapter of this book: one of *Nachträglichkeit* (*après coup*, "deferred action"). First, a "traumatic" exposure to the excesses—Mallarmean in hermetic density, Swiftian in aggressive virulence, Freudian in analytic acumen—of Lacan's prose; then, a patient reading of Laplanche's work; finally, a return to Lacan, between the lines of whose writings the outlines of many of Laplanche's analyses may be intuited.[1] Lacan, I would suggest, like the "trauma" Freud analyzes in the *Project* of 1895, can have full impact, attain "psychical"—or intellectual—"effectiveness" only *after the event (nachträglich)*.

Here we touch on some of the rare qualities of Laplanche's book. It is a study which was preceded by some five hundred pages of subtle prolegomena, written with J. B. Pontalis, under the title *Vocabulaire de la psychanalyse*.[2] That work was an extended effort to interpret the latent dynamics of Freud's thought as they become manifest in the difficulties posed by his terminology. *Life and Death* is Laplanche's own itinerary through that (reference) work, an effort to articulate precisely the most important lessons that may be learned from such an inquiry into Freud's terminology. As such, it is, I believe, deeply in accord with the general

---

[1] I have attempted to delineate the outline of the general structure of Laplanche's reading of Freud within Lacan's "Seminar on 'The Purloined Letter'" (trans. in *French Freud: Structural Studies in Psychoanalysis*, YFS 48 [New Haven, 1973]) in *"Poe pourri*: Lacan's Purloined Letter," *Semiotexte* 1, no. 3 (1975): 51–68.

[2] English translation by D. Micholson-Smith, *The Language of Psychoanalysis* (New York: Norton, 1974).

orientation of Lacan's reading of Freud, and yet it never invokes—or intimidates its readers with—the magisterial pronouncements of that author. More remarkably still, *Life and Death* ultimately never appeals to the authority of Freud himself. For what has authority in this reading is, in the final analysis, the perverse rigor with which a certain bizarre structure of Freud's text persistently plays havoc with the magisterial pronouncements—or authority—of Freud.

This last quality of Laplanche's work is of a piece with the central thesis in the book: that Freud's theory of repression, the heart of his discovery, was itself constantly and necessarily threatened with being repressed. Now that statement might strike a skeptical Anglo-American reader as the sheerest Parisian extravagance were it not for the precision of the analyses in this book. Laplanche is able to demonstrate that corresponding to each of a series of crucial Freudian terms—in a way that Freud plainly does not control—there are two different concepts at work. Moreover, in each of these conceptual pairs, one of the elements is solidary with a specific conceptual scheme and the other with a second one. That is, the conflict located in each term, however unintended or uncontrolled, functions systematically within the general economy of Freud's work. Indeed the entire body of Freud's *oeuvre* is constituted by Laplanche as an elaborately structured polemical field in which two mutually exclusive conceptual schemes may be seen to be struggling, as it were, to dominate—or cathect—a single terminological apparatus.

The reader will perhaps be best prepared to understand the workings of these two schemes, analyzed in detail in Laplanche's study, if we summarize briefly the organization of his book. In the first two chapters, we find a delineation of the processes whereby a bizarre form of culture or intersubjective exchange—"unconscious sexuality"—is generated in humans entirely through a movement of deviation from (natural) instinctual processes. (The key texts examined are the *Three Essays on the Theory of Sexuality* and the *Project for a Scientific Psychology*.) The second two chapters describe the genesis of an inhibiting or *repressive* agency within the subject: that stasis of libido known as the ego. Now the force and cogency of Laplanche's reading are a function of the discovery that the very movement whereby the theory of the repressive instance comes to be consolidated in Freud's thought—whereby a "narcissistic" agency is generated within his discourse—is inseparable from a repression of the—theory of what constitutes the—repressed. This process does not entail an abandonment of the terms mediating the analyses of the first two chapters, but rather an unwitting reassignment of new conceptual values to them, so that terms which were at first used to delineate a crucial discontinuity between a hypothetical "nature" and the uncanny "culture" of unconscious sexuality, and then between that form of "culture" and the illusory "nature" of a narcissistically constituted ego are, in the second scheme, made to articulate a theory of the maturational *continuum* leading genetically from archaic unconscious to an ego whose functions are synthesis, adaptation, and perception—the putative tasks of a living organism. What I have termed, all too concisely, the repression of the discovery of repression thus entails a shift of register from the ego of the theory of narcissism to the ego of (American) ego psychology, from a metaphorics of crucial discontinuity to one of vitalistic continualism. Finally, in the last two chapters, we find, in the analysis of the "death drive," the return of the theoretical "repressed," the affirmation of an *impossible* biological instance, which, in the intricacy of its structure, repeats, in displaced form, the new reality delineated in the first two chapters of the book. Thus a reading of Freud's writings on sado-masochism eludes the trap of regarding those texts as a phenomenology of perversion and succeeds in demonstrating how what had been lost, or repressed, through the processes delineated in the central two chapters is unwittingly regained in the final two.

It is perhaps tempting to regard the two conceptual schemes—roughly, "structuralist" vs. "functionalist," "discontinualist" vs. "continualist"—that we have described as struggling to invest Freud's terminological apparatus as equally valid interpretative possibilities for a reading of Freud's work. Indeed, one might even invoke "national temperament" and speak of quintessentially French and American interpretations of Freud. And yet we must insist on the ultimate untenability of such relativism. For the relation between the "American" scheme and the "French" one is that of a restricted economy and a general economy. More specifically, whereas the "American" (ego psychological) scheme thrives on its ignorance of the "French" one, the latter mediates nothing so much as an elaborate theory of the inevitability of the error entailed by the former. It will be sensed that at stake in Laplanche's reading is the immense American investment in its reading of Freud.

Finally, a word on translation. This book, with its scrupulous attention to terminology, is, of course, itself implicitly a treatise on the translation of Freud. Consequently, although Laplanche's lucid prose poses few problems for the translator, on almost every occasion on which he focuses on Freud's German, I have felt the necessity of either inflecting or modifying the English of the Standard Edition. For it is not the least exhilarating aspect of this work to provoke in the reader the disquieting sense that for reasons already manifest in the contradictions dividing the original text against itself, the principal thrust of Freud's theory may have been uncannily lost in translation. Such would be the superlatively paradoxical confirmation of Freud's theory of repression, and such as well the blinding resistance which Laplanche's remarkable analyses may help us to undo.

LIFE AND DEATH IN PSYCHOANALYSIS

Introduction

The six essays presented in this volume are a series of fragments or stages in a meditation on Freud's thought, undertaken in an effort to evolve—through a historico-structural approach to Freud's work—a problematics of the object of psychoanalysis.

If, concerning the discovery of psychoanalysis, I invoke the necessity of a certain historical approach, it is not in order to set out in pursuit of sources or influences, which may indeed account in part for a body of thought, nor to accord to chronology any other value than that of a convenient system of reference. The history—or the historical dimension—of psychoanalytic thought, as I understand it, can refer only to coordinates which are those of psychoanalysis itself. This is to say that in opposition to a manifest or official history (which Freud himself was occasionally intent on writing), such an enterprise would appeal to a latent and partially unconscious history, subtended by repetitive themes. This implies as well that it is inseparable from a certain dialectical approach, entailing an evolution through reversals and crises, mediated by contradictions whose status will not be immediately apparent in any attempt to situate them. Even if, in an interpretative stage, all the *contradictions* in Freud's thought are perhaps not amenable to the same treatment, not attributable to the same "mechanism" or "agency," they are all initially deserving of the same "free floating" attention. No doubt, in practice certain contradictions may prove to be relatively "extrinsic" or adventitious, the results of polemic or of hasty formulation; but even in such cases, they cannot be discarded without a certain loss. For, as we know from *The Interpretation of Dreams*, an absurdity in the manifest content or the secondary elaboration may be the index of a criticism or a difficulty at a deeper level. But it is above all certain large contradictions, traversing Freud's work from one end to the other, which must be interpreted dialectically, either as contradictions of thought—consequently referable to a certain "unspoken" dimension—or as contradictions of the object itself: such, for instance, is the case for the major contradiction inherent in the notion of the "ego," at once a totality and a

1

specific agency, a cathected love object that nevertheless arrogates to itself the position of a subject—and so on.

The contradictions in Freud's thought and the contradictions in his object are, in the final analysis, inseparable. But, in addition, their energy can be mobilized only if the problems or concepts concerning which they emerge are related both to the structural equilibrium in which those concepts find their point of insertion and to the propositions and the systems of oppositions in which they are engaged. The history of a notion which would neglect the structural perspective would result either in unfruitful absurdity, or in a reduction of the successive aspects of a thought to their lowest common denominator: the platitude on which most "treatises" of psychoanalysis seem intent. To cite but a single example, which we will have the opportunity to elaborate, it is impossible to discover, through Freud's occasionally awkward formulations, the meaning of the "pleasure principle," without taking into account the structural upheavals in which they find their place.[1]

Beyond the history of any specific problem then, I would sketch in these pages a history of the *overall* reorganizations of Freud's work, of the transition from a specific equilibrium to a structural imbalance and then to a different stage of his thought. A particularly decisive aspect of such a study would consist in showing how the major recastings of Freud's work (the famous "turning points") are correlated with the displacement of certain segments of his doctrine, conceptual groupings which one ought then to find in a different place and with a new function. Whence the ultimate question of knowing what finally motivates these reorganizations: the constraints of a structure and its equilibrium? The play of "cathexes" (i.e., the charges with which the author affects specific doctrinal elements, which then necessarily reemerge elsewhere if they are masked in their original locations)? Or is it the existence, in the final analysis, of a certain number of fundamental invariants, whether these be grouped under the rubric of intuition, of "Freud's discovery," or of a specific fundamental wish?

But might not the idea of a fundamental exigency—of an "invariancy" recurring throughout conceptual upheavals which are nevertheless astonishing—justify a radical critique of Freud's thought: if the essential was already there from the beginning (in the famous *Project for a Scientific Psychology* of 1895), the so-called recastings of Freud's work could be reduced to a kaleidoscopic play, to a series of permutations which would evoke less the evolution and enrichment of scientific thought than the versions of what Lévi-Strauss designates as "wild thought" (*la pensée sauvage*)?

An answer, which I can only sketch at this juncture, would be pursued on two levels. (1) Concerning empirical facts, it is easy to demonstrate the positive enhancement from which psychoanalytic doctrine, in the course of its evolution, has benefited as a result of *analytic experience*. But so obvious a truth, in turn, invites a different reflection: one ought to delineate the developmental model of a system of thought which, in certain aspects, appears to be *philosophical*, evolving according to its own inner necessity, whereas, on the other hand, it integrates in the manner of a *science* the new *data* afforded by a particularly rich field of observation. We are faced, then, with a unique meshing of theoretical thought and of experience, different in kind from any other because of one insuperable factor: the "internal" necessity of the doctrine and the "internal" impetus of what is revealed in therapeutic observation are grafted on a single root and intersect in the depth of a common "umbilicus." (2) At the level of content, the only answer consists in delineating the major and constant lines of the Freudian problematic, in order subsequently, taking one's distance from the author's own formulations, to attempt an *interpretation* of that problematic, which restores it to its most radical elements. Whereby is postulated the thesis that one can—in terms which at times repeat those of Freud and at times reverse them—reconstitute a structure of Freudian theory beyond the successive forms in which it is embodied.

It goes without saying that our approach to Freud's thought tends to deny that there exist within it moments of real "break" [*coupure*]. Without wanting to discuss that term—on which current fashion has seized—I hope to demonstrate that in Freud, throughout the changes in theory, it is the permanence of an exigency and the repetition of the journal of a discovery that are being expressed in a conceptualization which does not always succeed in immediately finding its adequate scientific form.

Interpreting Freud, rediscovering in him unconscious lines of force, is thus an approach dictated by its very object. But if I designate as "psychoanalytic" or "interpretative" this kind of study, it is not in the sense that an Ernest Jones conceives it in his biography of Freud, following methodological leads, it is true, already proposed by Freud himself. A Freudian text from 1911 ("The Claims of Psychoanalysis to Scientific Interest") gives several indications concerning the way in which one might conceive of the psychoanalytic approach to a philosophical work. Caught between a purely rational critique and a reduction of a body of thought to entirely "subjective" conditions, Freud proposes a skillful compromise: psychoanalysis puts its finger on the weak points of a theory, but it is left to internal criticism to demonstrate those weaknesses revealed by a different discipline.

I do not think that such is the last word concerning a psychoanalytic study of systematic thought, if it is true that what psychoanalysis discovers goes far beyond the realm of the individual and finds in the individual unconscious the figures, if not the solutions, of a more general combinatorial model. It is not, in any event, through any psychobiographical orientation that this work would be psychoanalytic. My study is first of all and essentially a study of Freud's text: at once *literal*, *critical*, and *interpretative*.

To the extent that it is literal and interpretative, this kind of approach to Freud is a necessarily tentative and imperfect effort to transpose *mutatis mutandis* what can be assimilated from the art of listening and interpreting in psychoanalytic therapy.[2] Thus the dual and complementary rule of free association and free-floating attention would find its equivalent in an "analytic" reading perpetually prepared to treat at the same level sequences of varying length: of words (even if they make no sense), of sentences, and of texts. Our interpretation ought then to draw on a knowledge of the unconscious mechanisms delineated by psychoanalysis: displacement, condensation, symbolization, which I have partially reformulated, in different coordinates, under the headings of metaphor and metonymy.[3]

Ours is a *critical* reading, however, to the extent that the style of each work, its location and destination require that it not be taken for granted, as a simple building block to be juxtaposed with others. If it is verifiable that psychoanalytic thought is constantly subject to the attraction of a kind of entropy, abrading its asperities to the lowest level, that vicissitude of psychoanalytic thought is already present in Freud, notably in the general presentations which he gave of his theory; so that it is unfair to the originality of his thought to base one's exposition of it essentially or entirely on one of the major synthetic texts.

It would be wrong to ignore the opposition that may exist between a critical intention and the analytic rule just invoked, which imposes on the practitioner—analyst or analysand—a suspension of judgment comparable in a sense, to "phenomenological reduction": the elimination of any selection among the "material." But I do not regard my attempt to combine or alternate these two contrary attitudes as unfaithful to the theory of the psychical apparatus, nor, for that matter, to certain inevitable aspects of psychoanalytic practice: when "secondary elaboration," an ego phenomenon, becomes all-pervasive, it may prove methodologically sound tentatively to disregard—in order to return better armed later on when the analysis has progressed—certain developments in which systematization attempts to block out any infiltration of the unconscious. It should, moreover, be admitted that with Freud as our object, one need never go that far: the most systematic text easily manifests its permeability to the life of the unconscious, upon contact with the essays, sketches, and speculative experiments through which it is ramified.

I have attempted to present my interpretation *as such* and to specify with precision its contours, while at the same time justifying it as a nascent tendency of Freud's work to interpret itself. Thereby I hope to define my effort in relation to two contrary "interpretative" attitudes. One of these consists in assimilating all of Freud's pronouncements to one's own position, through a series of slippages which are never acknowledged as such. The other attitude, more faithful no doubt, does not, however, do full justice to the originality of Freud's thought in the unity of its emergence: it would sort out the wheat from the chaff in order to use the former in its own "bread," but it risks, in so doing, limiting itself largely to the most classical, most official, and least inspired level of Freud's doctrine.

II

It occurred to me that the sequence of these essays, grouped around the classical notion of conflict, outlined the network of a more complex problematic: the intervention of the vital order and of death at the periphery of the domain of psychoanalysis and also—according to what modalities?—within that domain.

Life and death: two terms which are present in analytic theory, occasionally with striking prominence, but which are far more concealed in practice. From the "exigencies of life" of the *Project* of 1895 and the unconditional adoption, during the period of the "transference" with Fliess, of the doctrine of "periods" and bisexuality, to the life instinct, which, at the end of Freud's work, comes to subsume sexuality, biology and biologism are massively present in the author's writings. Is it simply a matter of the contiguity of an immediately adjacent domain, concerning which, retroactively, discoveries regarding instinctual life and sexuality would allow one to renew one's point of view? Such is the "interdisciplinary" approach that Freud explicitly[4]—and Jones in his wake[5]—proposes in defining the contribution of psychoanalysis to biology: a contribution concerning which it should indeed be noted that it still awaits accomplishment. As for the converse: the intervention of the life sciences in psychoanalysis is frequently invoked by Freud as decisive, notably in reference to the theory of drives, but the fact that that invocation most often refers to the speculative or poetic demons of biologism should give us pause.

If life, despite these reservations, is regarded as materially present at the frontiers of the psyche, death's entry on the Freudian scene is far more enigmatic. In the beginning, like all modalities of the negative, it is radically excluded from the field of the unconscious. Then suddenly in 1920, it emerges at the center of the system, as one of the two fundamental forces—and perhaps even as the only primordial force—in the heart of the psyche, of living beings, and of matter itself. The soul of conflict, an elemental form of strife, which from then on is in the forefront of Freud's most theoretical formulations, death nevertheless remains, most often, a silent personage in clinical practice. For Freud maintains until the end the strictest reservations concerning the developments which, almost naturally, his new conceptualization would seem to invite: the occurrence of "death anxiety" or of an originary wish to die will never be located, in analytic psychopathology, in that position of irreducible "bedrock" which is attributed par excellence to the castration complex.

Might it be that death—human death as finitude and not the sole reduction to zero of vital tensions—finds its place, in psychoanalysis, in a dimension which is more ethical than explanatory? A text[6]—a single text—published only five years before "Beyond the Pleasure Principle," might lead one to suppose so, at least from its first lines. Appearing to join up with that heroic and classical current which, from the Stoics to Montaigne and Heidegger, urges us to illuminate our life—our existence —with a deathly light, "Thoughts for the Times on War and Death" would recall in concluding that "the bearing of life is the first duty of every living being," and invite us to transpose the old adage "If you seek peace, prepare for war" into "Si vis vitam para mortem." This maxim Freud, yielding perhaps to the temptation of his subject, translates: "If you would endure life, be prepared for death." Thus: for *your* death.

That is, however, a conclusion which follows, without any other justification, a development that is oriented quite differently: "Our unconscious is just as inaccessible to the idea of our own death, as murderously minded towards the stranger, as divided or ambivalent towards the loved, as was man in earliest antiquity."[7]

In the unconscious, death would be always the death of the other, a destruction or a loss we provoke, and we would accede to some intuition of our own mortality only through an ambivalent identification with a loved person whose death we simultaneously fear and desire: essentially in mourning. So that, more modestly perhaps in relation to the temptations of the heroic formulation, "If you want life, prepare for death" might be translated as "If you want life, prepare for the death of the other." If a certain ethic in relation to death might be evolved from the Freudian attitude, it would be in the sense of a distrust concerning every form of enthusiasm, be it that of *amor fati*, and of a lucidity that does not hide the irreducible meshing of my death with that of the other. The seal of authenticity that marks Freud's "necrological notes" or "condolence" letters reflects only the pursuit of a self-analysis which was never abandoned.

Which is to say that in therapy—although it can be defined in no other way than as an unveiling of truth—ultimately a reference to death as the truth of life or as the experience of truth can only be regarded as an uninterpretable, axiomatic limit-element. The suspension of every "purposive idea" concerns as well, and perhaps first of all, what is defined in *Beyond the Pleasure Principle* as "the final purpose of life." And if one can perhaps discover within therapy other ways in which death comes to be represented, they are not necessarily to be sought on the side of "representation" or "ideation" but in a certain immanence of discourse itself.

Refracted or represented in quite diverse ways, neither life nor death are thus direct terms of reference for psychoanalytic practice. That remark may serve as well as a warning: an interrogation—without precaution—of the psychoanalytic act, with reference to a conception of existence which (pessimistically or optimistically) relates human life to its finitude, would constitute, from the beginning, a refusal to take into account that calling into question necessitated by the discovery of the unconscious and of the shifts occurring within it. Not that I would reject definitively any consideration of the dimension of a "project" in its relation to psychoanalysis. But I believe that the bases of such a discussion would have to be previously prepared by a study pursuing Freud's deliberately theoretical intention when he introduces into psychoanalysis the biological polarity of life and death, and that such an inquiry, prolonging Freud's indications by interpreting them, should attempt to retrace the vicissitudes of the vital order (life and death) when it is transposed to the level of the psychical apparatus.

We shall follow this transformation into something different that life undergoes when it symbolizes itself on the human level in three movements that will lead us to examine successively the problematics of sexuality, of the ego, and of the death drive.

1

The Order of Life and the Genesis of Human Sexuality

Our point of reference in discussing sexuality in psychoanalysis will be Freud's fundamental and resolutely innovative text *Three Essays on the Theory of Sexuality*. The importance the author attributed to that work is manifest in the frequency with which he modified it: in reeditions of 1910, 1915, 1920, and 1924–25, revised on each occasion in the very detail of its sentences and terminology, with additions which simultaneously preserve the original organization of the work and open it up to later discoveries. There are, in addition, copious notes, particularly for the final, 1924 version, which is contemporaneous with the "last theory of drives." It is in these strata and repetitions that the evolution and enrichment of the theory of sexuality may be best situated. But since we have just alluded to a last turning point, the final version—in the sense in which a "version" constitutes as well a way of reversing a work, a turning point—that final version, begun in 1920, is inscribed only minimally in the text itself, with the exception of the footnotes. So that if one wanted an approximate idea of what the *Three Essays* might have been had they been first undertaken in 1920, one would do best to consult a text like the *Outline of Psychoanalysis* (1938), and specifically its third chapter. And yet even in so late a text as the *Outline*, one senses the immense difficulty experienced by Freud in proposing a synthesis, as though his final contribution—concerning Eros and the death drive—could but barely be integrated into the first notion of sexuality.

For the *Three Essays* do not present an abstract theory of drives in general, but describe instead that drive par excellence: the sexual drive. So much so, in fact, that without pretending to remain faithful (through some falsely eclectic synthesis) to the *entirety* of what Freud may have said concerning drives, we may claim, nevertheless, to follow the dominant line of his thought in offering a thesis which will recur throughout our argument: *it is sexuality which represents the model of every drive and probably constitutes the only drive in the strict sense of the term.* And

8

if it is indeed true that, after 1920, Freud proposes and supports a theory englobing *two types* of drives, and links sexuality with one of them—with that biological, even cosmological force he then calls Eros—it is at that point that our thesis will seem most openly in contradiction with Freud's thought, but it is precisely at that juncture as well that a series of difficulties will also surface in Freud's own work.

In our first development, we will confine ourselves to sexuality as it constitutes the object of the *Three Essays*. In any effort to grasp what is, in fact, at stake in that text, nothing is more instructive than a glance at its organization: an apparently simple scheme, in three parts: sexual aberrations, infantile sexuality, the transformations of puberty. And yet were one to reconstitute a detailed table of contents, the greatest complication would result. That complexity is, of course, in part due to interpolations dating from different kinds of arrangement: a level one might term heuristic (following the genesis of psychoanalytic discovery itself), a polemical level (destroying the accepted conception of sexuality), a genetic level (retracing its emergence within the human being). We shall attempt to delineate how these three different levels may be articulated, how specifically the movement of Freud's thought, the heuristic level, follows—as in every profound exercise of thought—the movement of the "thing itself": a truth it was Hegel's to have rendered explicit.

The guiding thread in our study will be the notion of *drive* (*Trieb*), and the pair it forms with a second term: *instinct*. If it is true in general that terminology, and above all its transposition from one language to another, can guide—but also misguide—us, problems of translation have introduced in the present case a confusion which is far from having disappeared. Whence our concern that the following remarks not be attributed simply to the meticulousness of a translator. *Trieb* has frequently been translated in French as *instinct*, and transposed by psychoanalysts in English, as well, as *instinct*. Yet we encounter in Freud, and in the German language in general, not one but two terms, two "signifiers," to use a more recent terminology. Two signifiers then, and it may be said that in common usage they have more or less the same meaning, just as their etymologies are parallel: *Trieb* comes from *treiben*, "to push"; *Instinkt* finds its origin in Latin, from *instinguere*, which also means "to incite," "to push." But—as is frequently the case with languages and especially with German—when faced with a doublet of this type, an author approaching latent inflections of vocabulary with all the seriousness they deserve will attempt to exploit such objective duplicity in order to introduce a slight difference of meaning, which is occasionally barely perceptible, but will at times be accentuated to the point of constituting a veritable opposition. Such is the case with *Trieb* ("drive") and *Instinkt* ("instinct"): two terms which are employed by Freud even if, unfortunately, it has been insufficiently noted that the term *Instinkt* is used to designate something entirely different from what is described elsewhere as sexuality. *Instinkt*, in Freud's language, is a preformed behavioral pattern, whose arrangement is determined hereditarily and which is repeated according to modalities relatively adapted to a certain type of object. More important than etymology then, more important even than their semantic resonances in German culture, we discover a certain relation between meanings assumed by the two terms in Freud's scientific discovery, a complex relation, comprising an *analogy*, a *difference*, and also a *derivation* from one to the other. This is a derivation which is not simply conceptual, but which we may, with Freud, relate to a real derivation: the derivation in man of drives from instincts.[1]

First their analogy: it is based on a common substrate in the analysis of the concept. The analysis of a drive, as it is presented to us in its elements, is also valid, in its generality, for an instinct. That analysis is sketched out, through successive approximations, in the course of different editions of the *Three Essays*, but in order to find a more systematic presentation, one had best consult a later text, "Instincts and Their Vicissitudes."[2] There, the drive is decomposed according to four dimensions or, as Freud puts it, according to the four "terms which are used in reference to the concept of a drive": "impetus" (*Drang*), "aim" (*Ziel*), "object" (*Objekt*), and "source" (*Quelle*).

The *impetus*, he first tell us, is the motor factor in the drive, "the amount of force or the measure of the demand for work which it represents. The character of exercising pressure is common to all drives; it is in fact their very essence." These lines are exemplary in their reference to mechanics and, more precisely, to dynamics, which will always remain central for Freud. What is called the economic point of view in psychoanalysis is quite precisely that of a "demand for work": if there is work, a modification in the organism, it is because ultimately there is an exigency, a force; and, as in the physical sciences, force can be defined only through the measure of a quantity of work. To define a drive by its impetus, a *Trieb* by its *Drang*, is, from an epistemological point of view, almost a tautology: the latter is but the hypostasized, abstract element of the former. So that, to anticipate what will follow, we would propose the following hypothesis: it is that abstract element alone, the economic factor, which will remain constant in the derivation that will bring us from instincts to drives.

The *aim* now. It is, Freud tells us in the *Three Essays*, "the act to which the drive is driven." Thus, in the case of a preformed instinct, it is the motory scheme, the series of acts which results in a certain accomplishment. What precisely is that accomplishment? If we refer this time to the text "Instincts and Their Vicissitudes," we see that this accomplishment is always the same and ultimately rather monotonous; the only "final" aim is always satisfaction, defined in the most general way: the appeasing of a certain tension caused precisely by the *Drang*, that pressure we have been speaking about. The question then arises of determining the relation between an aim which is entirely general and (as with "impetus") abstract—the appeasing of tension—and, on the other hand, the very specific and determined acts which are the aims of various instincts: eating, seeing (since one finds in Freud a "drive to see"), making love, etc. The problem is that of the specification of the aim: why is it that something quite specific and not simply appeasement represents the *final aim*?

If we pursue the analysis, drawing on different texts of Freud, we discover that the aim of the drive constantly calls into play the following two factors: at times the object, at others, the source. The *object*: to the extent that Freud and, after him, virtually all psychoanalysts gradually came to focus on the notion of "object relations," which represents a kind of synthetic point of view between, on the one hand, a type of activity, the specific mode of a particular drive action, and on the other, its privileged object. Thus orality, to take the first example of a drive, implies both a certain mode of relation, say incorporation, and a certain type of object, one which is capable of being swallowed or incorporated. We encounter here a first possible elaboration of the notion of aim, its specification by its *source*; and here, apparently (we will soon see that the theory is in fact more complex) a far more biologistic and vitalistic orientation seems to prevail.

We shall examine, then, in greater detail these two concepts: *object* and *source*. Object of the drive? In order to eliminate rapidly certain misconceptions, we shall recall first that such an object is not necessarily an inanimate one, a thing: the Freudian *Objekt* is not opposed in essence to subjective being. No "objectification" of the love relation is intended. If in the classical language of the French seventeenth century, the term was already used to designate the focus of passion—*flamme, ressentiment*—it is in that rather broad sense that our "object" should be understood. And yet our caution against a vulgarized concept of the love object ("You treat me like an object," as the phrase goes) should not be taken as absolute. One perceives this simply by following the movement of its "definition" in the *Three Essays*. Temporarily, in the introduction, the "sexual object" is defined as "the person from whom sexual attraction proceeds."[3] But the analysis of sexual aberrations results in an inversion of this point of view:

It has been brought to our notice that we have been in the habit of regarding the connection between the sexual drive and the sexual object as more intimate than it in fact is. Experience of the cases that are considered abnormal has shown us that in them the sexual instinct and the sexual object are merely soldered together—a fact which we have been in danger of overlooking in consequence of the uniformity of the normal picture, where the object appears to form part and parcel of the drive. We are thus warned to loosen the bond that exists in our thoughts between drive and object. It seems probable that the sexual drive is in the first instance independent of its object; nor is its origin likely to be due to its object's attractions.[4]

Thus, despite our reservations, the term *object* appears initially to designate something which functions as a means: "the thing in regard to which or through which the drive is able to achieve its aim."[5] There is a priority of satisfaction and of the satisfying action in relation to that "in regard to which" that action finds its conclusion. This brings us to a familiar problem in psychoanalytic thought, which might be termed summarily the "contingency" of the object. Insofar as the object is that "in which" the aim finds its realization, the specificity or individuality of the object is, after all, of minimal concern; it is enough for it to possess certain *traits* which trigger the satisfying action; in itself, it remains relatively indifferent and contingent.

An additional dimension of the object in psychoanalysis is that it is not necessarily an object in the sense of the theory of knowledge: an "objective" object. We might here distinguish clearly two meanings which unfortunately, in recent psychoanalytic theory, are too often in a state of coalescence: the notion of objectivity in the sense of knowledge and the notion of objectality in which the object, this time, is an object of the drive and not a scientific or perceptual object. I point this out in order to emphasize that the object of the drive can be, without prejudice, a *fantasmatic* object and that it is perhaps essentially such.

Finally, to conclude this series of clarifications, we should insist that the object is not necessarily a "total" person; it may be a *partial* (or *component*) object, in the phrase introduced by Melanie Klein but found—and quite early—at the center of Freud's thought. Partial objects include breast, penis, and numerous other elements related to bodily life (excrement, child, etc.), all of which have in common the fundamental characteristic of being, in fact or in fantasy, *detached* or *detachable*.

In concluding this analysis of the notion of *drive*, we will focus our attention at greater length on the term *source*. If, in the *Three Essays*, the definition of a source—as we shall soon see—is relatively complex and ambiguous, in the text "Instincts and Their Vicissitudes," to which reference has been made collaterally, it is univocal: the *Quelle* is an unknown but theoretically knowable somatic process, a kind of biological *x*, whose psychical translation would in fact be the drive. By the "source of a drive" is meant "that somatic process in an organ or part of the body from which there results a stimulus represented in mental life by a drive."[6] We note here the term *represented*, a fundamental articulation of Freud's metapsychology, which the limits of this presentation do not allow us to elaborate: suffice it to observe that the most frequent model used by Freud to account for the relation between the somatic and the psychical employs the metaphor of a kind of "delegation" provided with a mandate that need not be absolutely imperative. Thus a local biological stimulus finds its delegation, its "representation" in psychical life as a drive. We do not know whether the somatic process in question is of a strictly chemical nature, or whether it corresponds as well to a release of other (e.g., mechanical) forces: the study of the sources of drives, Freud concludes, "lies outside the scope of psychology," and the problem might eventually be solved by biology.[7] Thus we encounter the central problem of our own study: the relation to the science of life.

We shall return in a moment to the question of the source, which seems particularly interesting as the point of articulation between instinct and drive. In the interim, before examining that *articulation*, we shall insist first on the analogy which exists, concerning our four "elements," between an instinct and a drive; or rather, in other words, we shall underscore the generality of the definitions of impetus, object, aim, and source, a generality which allows them to be applied to *both* instincts and drives. Such is, I believe, the wager implicit in "Instincts and Their Vicissitudes," and such as well is the trap that text sets for the unprepared reader: the essay would examine drives *in general*, not simply sexual drives but all those "groups" of drives—including consequently the "ego-drives" or "self-preservative drives"—concerning which we shall shortly have to ask whether the name *drive* is in fact properly applied to them. To deal with every *Trieb* in general is necessarily to proceed in an abstract manner. To deal with drives in general is to biologize them, to subject them to an analysis which is *also* valid for so-called instinctual patterns of behavior. As evidence, one need but invoke the validity of such concepts in recent analyses in the fields of animal psychology or ethology. The research of contemporary animal psychologists, specifically in Lorenz's school, makes extensive use, even if reference is not regularly made to Freud, of concepts analogous to his; specifically, the notion of "impetus" is employed, since the *hydraulic model*, which is most often invoked by Freud to account for the economic factor, is expressly adopted by them. The notion of an object which would simultaneously be contingent and, from a certain point of view, specific is present in the notion of a perceptual constellation triggering a specific act, and capable of releasing a specific mechanism because it includes a series of determined traits. As is known, it is by the use of perceptual lures, whose different characteristics are made to vary, that certain of these triggers have been precisely defined. Finally, the notion of an *aim* is also present in ethological analysis in the form of a fixed behavioral pattern, a series of chain reactions ending in a permanent discharge of tension: a cycle which may stop at any particular stage if the succeeding triggering device is not present to provoke the corresponding mechanism.

Having insisted on the *general* value of Freud's definitions, a generality which includes both a negative aspect (since the definitions may appear abstract) but also a positive one (since these notions can be shown to coincide with those of a science as concretely empirical as ethology), we shall return to the *Three Essays*, and to their very first page, on which is found a succinct description of the "popular" conception of sexuality. The *Three Essays* begin:

> The fact of the existence of sexual needs in human beings and animals is expressed in biology by the assumption of a "sexual drive," on the analogy of the instinct of nutrition, that is, of hunger. Everyday language possesses no counterpart to the word "hunger," but science makes use of the word "libido" for that purpose.
>
> Popular opinion has quite definite ideas about the nature and characteristics of this sexual drive. It is generally understood to be absent in childhood, to set in at the time of puberty in connection with the process of coming to maturity and to be revealed in the manifestations of an irresistible attraction exercised by one sex upon the other; while its aim is presumed to be sexual union, or at all events actions leading in that direction.[8]

This "popular" conception is, at the same time, a biologizing conception in which sexuality, the sexual *drive*, is conceived of on the model of an *instinct*, a response to a natural need whose paradigm is hunger (if we may be allowed at this point to make more systematic use than Freud of the conceptual pair drive-instinct). In the case of sexuality, this need would appear to be grounded in a process of maturation, a process of strictly internal origin, in which the physiological moment of puberty is determinant; it would thus be a behavioral sequence narrowly determined by its "source," with a fixed and quite precise "object," since sexuality would focus uniquely and in a manner predetermined for all eternity on the other sex; finally, its "aim" would be similarly fixed: "sexual union, or at all events actions leading in that direction." We should, then, insist on the fact that this "popular conception," which Freud summarizes here in order to expose it subsequently to his attack, coincides with an image which may seem scientific, in the sense of a science of life, an image which, in the last analysis, is perhaps quite valid, at least in domains *other* than that of human sexuality. If we return now to the organization of the *Three Essays*, we shall understand better how that organization is modeled, in its movement, on the very object of the work: the entire organization may be understood as a function of a certain "destruction" (perhaps in the sense of Hegel's *Aufhebung*) of this "popular"—but also biologizing—image of sexuality. There are three chapters, as we recalled earlier. The first is "Sexual Aberrations," and we might subtitle that first chapter "The

Instinct Lost." The second chapter is entitled "Sexuality," and we elaborate: "The Genesis of Human Sexuality." Finally, the third chapter, "The Transformations of Puberty"; perhaps then, in a sense, the instinct regained? No doubt, but regained at a different level. Rather than *regained*, we would propose provisionally a formula such as "The Instinct Mimed."

We shall treat the first *Essay* only briefly, and in order to situate the second, which is the principal focus of this chapter. It presents us with a polemical, almost apologetic catalogue of sexual aberrations. At stake is an effort to destroy received notions of a *specific aim* and *specific object* through a description of perversions. It is a presentation, moreover, which is distinguished neither by its scientific rigor nor by the exhaustiveness of its explanations. There is no basis for seeking in the *Three Essays* the alpha—and certainly not the omega—of the psychoanalytic theory of the perversions. The crux for Freud is to show just how extended, almost universal, the field of perversions is, and how their existence demolishes any idea of a determined aim or object for human sexuality. Sexuality, one might say upon reading this first chapter, gives the appearance, in a so-called normal adult, of an instinct, but that is only the precarious result of a historical evolution which at every stage of its development may bifurcate differently, resulting in the strangest aberrations.

Our consideration of the second *Essay* will center on a passage which delineates the essence of the matter in that it redefines sexuality as a function of its infantile origins. I refer to the conclusion of a section entitled "The Manifestations of Infantile Sexuality":

> Our study of thumb-sucking or sensual sucking [taken as a model of oral sexuality] has already given us the three essential characteristics of an infantile sexual manifestation. At its origin it *attaches itself to* [*or props itself upon; entsteht in Anlehnung an*] one of the vital somatic functions; it has as yet no sexual object, and is thus *auto-erotic*; and its sexual aim is dominated by an *erotogenic zone*.[9]

We should observe straightaway that these three characteristics are found in most erotic manifestations of childhood and that they even transcend in large measure the sexuality of the *age* of childhood, marking definitively the entirety of human sexuality. The definition invokes three original and complex notions: the notion of *propping*, the notion of *auto-erotism*; finally, the notion of an *erotogenic zone*.

Propping [*Etayage*], the French reader will perhaps be surprised to hear, is a fundamental term in Freud's conceptual apparatus. In current translations of Freud, in French as well as in the excellent Standard Edition in English, the only trace of the Freudian concept is the sporadic and poorly justified use of an adjective derived from the Greek: "anaclitic." A prolonged consideration of Freudian terminology[10] and an effort

at retranslating Freud's work have led us to choose, along with the
original French translator who had already used it unsystematically, the
term *étayage* (*propping*) and its derivatives. If we have adopted that term,
it is because it was necessary to bring into focus, as had not been done
before, the rigorous conceptual value which the German word *Anlehnung*—meaning "to find support" or propping in something else—takes
on in Freud. We have attempted thereby to bring into relief with its
various resonances a notion long obscured by translations more concerned with elegance than rigor, specifically by an excessively learned and
insufficiently explicit pseudoscientific term: *anaclisis*. In addition, the
adjective *anaclitic* had in turn been inflected by an elaborate psychoanalytic tradition originating in a point which is already, in fact, secondary.
For the term *anaclitic* was introduced by the translators in a text later
than the *Three Essays*, the essay "On Narcissism" (1914), in which Freud
contrasts two types of "object choice," two ways in which the human
subject selects his love object: a "narcissistic" object choice, in which man
chooses his love object in his own image, and an "anaclitic" object choice
(*Anlehnungstypus*, in the German) in which (such at least is how the
matter was a bit hastily interpreted) one's sexuality is based on the object
of the function of self-preservation. Thus the term *propping* has been
understood in this tradition as a leaning on the *object*, and ultimately a
leaning on the mother. It may thus be intuited how an elaborate theory of
a relation with the mother has come to inflect a notion intended to
account for sexuality in its emergence. In fact, if one examines that notion
more closely, one sees that originally it by no means designates a leaning
of the subject on the object (of child on mother), even if such "leaning" is
observable elsewhere. The phenomenon Freud describes is a leaning *of
the drive*, the fact that emergent sexuality attaches itself to and is propped
upon another process which is both similar and profoundly divergent: the
sexual drive is propped upon a nonsexual, vital function or, as Freud
formulates it in terms which defy all additional commentary, upon a
"bodily function essential to life." It will thus be admitted that our
divergence from Freud's thought is minimal, that we are in fact only
rendering it more precise when we say that what is described as propping
is a *leaning originally* of infantile sexuality on the instincts, if by instinct is
meant that which orients the "bodily function essential to life"; in the
particular case first analyzed by Freud, the instinct is hunger and the
function feeding. Without the terminological coherence of Freud's writings being absolutely systematic, we shall nevertheless find, in a manner
sufficiently motivated to allow us in turn to "lean" upon it, that the terms
function, *need*, and *instinct* characterize generally the vital register of self-
preservation in opposition to the sexual register.

With the *propping of the drive on the function*, we are faced not with an abstract genesis, a quasi-metaphysical deduction, but with a process that is described with the utmost precision in the archetypal example of orality. In orality, it is shown, two phases may be delineated: one consisting in sucking of the breast, and a second, quite different from the first, which is characterized as "sensual sucking." In the first phase —breast-sucking for nourishment—we are faced with a function or, to recall our earlier distinction, with a total instinctual pattern of behavior, one which is, in fact, so complete, as we have seen, that it is precisely hunger, the feeding pattern, which the "popular conception" assumes to be the *model of every instinct.* It is an instinctual pattern with its "impetus," and this time we should be able to specify precisely what may be hidden behind the energetic x term and, drawing on psychophysiology, to relate to a specific humoral or tissual imbalance that state of tension corresponding subjectively to the impression of hunger. We thus have an "impetus," an accumulation of tensions; a "source" as well, the digestive system, with—to localize and restrict things further—those points in which appetite is most specifically felt. A specific "object" is similarly introduced into the discussion. Shall we identify it as the breast? Well, no, since it is not the breast which procures satisfaction but the nourishment: milk. Finally, there is a preformed process or "aim," that process of breast-sucking which observers have undertaken to describe with great precision: the search for the nipple, feeding, the release of tension, pacification.

Now the crucial point is that simultaneous with the feeding function's achievement of satisfaction in nourishment, a sexual process begins to appear. Parallel with feeding there is a stimulation of lips and tongue by the nipple and the flow of warm milk. This stimulation is initially modeled on the function, so that between the two, it is at first barely possible to distinguish a difference. The object? It would appear to be furnished at the level of the function. Can we be sure whether it is still the milk or already the breast? The source? It too is determined by the feeding process, since lips are also part of the digestive system. The aim as well is quite close to the aim of nourishment. Ultimately object, aim, and source are intimately entwined in an extremely simple proposition allowing us to describe the process: "It's coming in by the mouth." "It" is the object; "coming in" is the aim, and whether a sexual or an alimentary aim is in question, the process is in any event a "coming in"; "by the mouth": at the level of the source, we find the same duplicity: the mouth is simultaneously a sexual organ and an organ of the feeding function.

Thus the "propping" consists initially in that support which emergent sexuality finds in a function linked to the preservation of life. We can find no better conclusion than the following quotation of another passage Freud devotes to the oral-erotic activity of the child:

It is also easy to guess the occasions on which the child had his first experiences of the pleasure which he is now striving to renew. It was the child's first and most vital activity, his sucking at his mother's breast, or at substitutes for it, that must have familiarized him with this pleasure. The child's lips, in our view, behave like an *erotogenic zone*, and no doubt stimulation by the warm flow of milk is the cause of the pleasurable sensation. The satisfaction of the erotogenic zone is associated, in the first instance, with the satisfaction of the need for nourishment. To begin with, sexual activity attaches itself to [props itself upon] functions serving the purpose of self-preservation and does not become independent of them until later. No one who has seen a baby sinking back satiated from the breast and falling asleep with flushed cheeks and a blissful smile can escape the reflection that this picture persists as a prototype of the expression of sexual satisfaction in later life. The need for repeating the sexual satisfaction now becomes detached from the need for taking nourishment.[11]

In the very act of feeding, the process of propping may be revealed in a culminating satisfaction that already resembles orgasm; but above all, in an immediately subsequent phase, we witness a separation of the two, since sexuality, at first entirely grounded in the function, is simultaneously entirely *in the movement which disassociates it* from the vital function. In fact, the prototype of oral sexuality is not in the sucking of the breast, and is not, in all its generality, the activity of sucking [*succion*] but rather what Freud, drawing on the works of Lindner, calls *das Ludeln oder Lutschen* [*suçotement*]. Henceforth, the object is abandoned, the aim and the source also take on autonomy in relation to the activity of feeding and the digestive system. With "sensual sucking" we thus come to the second "characteristic" referred to above, which is also a "moment" intimately linked to the process of propping which precedes it: auto-erotism.

Auto-erotism: Freud borrows the term from the sexologists of his time, notably Havelock Ellis, but he brings to it a new import: He defines it essentially in terms of the absence of an object (*Objektlösigkeit*): "a sexual activity . . . not directed towards other people." Now that definition prompts us to indicate immediately that if the notion of auto-erotism will fulfill an extremely important function in Freud's thought, it will simultaneously lead to a major aberration in psychoanalytic thinking and, perhaps, to a certain aberration in the thought of Freud himself, concerning the "object" and primal absence of the object. In such a perspective the object would be generated as it were *ex nihilo*, by a stroke of some magic wand, from an initial state regarded as totally "objectless." The human individual must thus "open up" to his world—things as well as individuals—starting from what we are tempted to call a state of biological idealism, no doubt even more inconceivable than philosophical solipsism. Deriving an object from an objectless state seems so unpromising a theoretical task to certain analysts that they do not hesitate to affirm—in a reaction which is laudable in its intentions but which only leads to a different error—that *sexuality per se* has an object from the beginning. Such is the position of a psychoanalytic author like Balint who undertakes, with frequently attractive arguments, to demonstrate that a "primary object love" in the child exists,[12] so successfully, in fact, that henceforth all psychoanalytic discussion concerning the object has been restricted to the following alternative: either a total absence of objects for the human being, or the presence from the beginning of a *sexual* object. What path shall we take to avoid this false impasse? The solution is indicated on several occasions, in passages corresponding to moments of particular lucidity in Freud's thought. If we say "particular lucidity," it is out of a sense that certain discoveries may be forgotten, eclipsed, or repressed by their author: there are clear examples in the case of Freud himself, and notably concerning the point under consideration.

The following is a crucial passage, located further on, in the third *Essay*, but which summarizes the theses of the second *Essay*:

At a time at which the first beginnings of sexual satisfaction are still linked with the taking of nourishment [i.e., in the propping phase], the sexual instinct has a sexual object outside the infant's own body in the shape of his mother's breast. It is only later that he loses it, just at the time, perhaps, when he is able to form a total idea of the person to whom the organ that is giving him satisfaction belongs. As a rule the sexual drive then becomes auto-erotic [*auto-erotism is thus not the initial stage*], and not until the period of latency has been passed through is the original relation restored. There are thus good reasons why a child sucking at his mother's breast has become the prototype of every relation of love. The finding of an object is in fact a re-finding of it.[13]

The text cited has an entirely different ring to it from that vast fable of autoerotism as a state of the primary and total absence of an object: a state which one leaves in order to *find* an object; autoerotism is, on the contrary, a second stage, the stage of the loss of the object. A loss of the "partial" object, it should be noted, since it is a loss of the breast which is being considered, and Freud introduces at this point the precious observation that perhaps the partial object is lost at the moment in which the total object—the mother as person—begins to emerge. But above all, if such a text is to be taken seriously, it means that *on the one hand there is from the beginning an object, but that on the other hand sexuality does not have, from the beginning, a real object.* It should be understood that the real object, milk, was the object of the function, which is virtually preordained to the world of satisfaction. Such is the real object which has been lost, but the object linked to the autoerotic turn, the breast—become a fantasmatic breast—is, for its part, the object of the sexual drive. Thus the sexual object is not identical to the object of the function, but is displaced in relation to it; they are in a relation of essential *contiguity* which leads us to slide almost indifferently from one to the other, from the milk to the breast as its symbol. "The finding of an object," Freud concludes in a formulation that has since become famous, "is in fact a re-finding of it." We would elucidate this as follows: the object to be rediscovered is not the lost object, but its substitute by displacement; the lost object is the object of self-preservation, of hunger, and the object one seeks to refind in sexuality is an object displaced in relation to that first object. From this, of course, arises the impossibility of ultimately ever rediscovering the object, since the object which has been lost *is not the same* as that which is to be rediscovered. Therein lies the key to the essential "duplicity" situated at the very beginning of the sexual quest.

The sexual *aim* is, similarly, in a quite special position in relation to the aim of the feeding function; it is simultaneously the same and different. The aim of feeding was ingestion; in psychoanalysis, however, the term used is "incorporation." The terms may seem virtually identical, and yet there is a slight divergence between the two. With incorporation, the aim has become the scenario of a fantasy, a scenario borrowing from the function its register and its language, but adding to ingestion the various implications grouped under the term "cannibalism," with such meanings as: preserving within oneself, destroying, assimilating. Incorporation, moreover, extends ingestion to an entire series of possible relations; ingestion is no longer limited to food, since one can conceive of incorporation occurring in other bodily systems than the digestive apparatus: reference is thus made in psychoanalysis to incorporation at the level of other bodily orifices, of the skin or even, for instance, of the eyes. To speak of a visual incorporation may allow for the interpretation of certain symptoms. Thus from the aim of the function to the sexual aim, a transition exists which may still be defined in terms of a certain kind of displacement: one which, this time, follows an analogical or metaphorical line, and no longer an associative chain through contiguity.

Finally, before leaving the vicissitudes of the aim in the process of propping, we should note, alongside the fantasmatic scenario or activity (incorporation, in the case of orality), a second kind of aim, no doubt linked to the scenario but much more localized, much less "dialectical": that of a "pleasure taken on the spot," the sheer enjoyment of sensual sucking. Between the fantasmatic aim of incorporation and the far more local and far less subtle aim of stimulating the lips, there is necessarily a complex relation that we shall have to reexamine.

There remains the problem of the *source*. We noted earlier that this is perhaps the central question if what we are presently studying is indeed the *origin*, thus precisely *the source of sexuality*. It should be emphasized that this is not simply a word game, neither for us nor for Freud, since we encounter in the *Three Essays* two meanings of the word *source*, with a relation between the two we should do well to follow. In an initial stage, *source* is taken in the most concrete and local sense of the term: as an erotogenic zone (to continue with the example of orality, the labial zone stimulated by the passage of milk). It is as though a biological scheme existed which would secrete sexuality from certain predetermined zones, exactly as certain physiological setups give rise to the need for nourishment through certain local tensions; we thus find the idea of a source in a strictly physiological sense. But we find as well a second meaning of the term, which is at least as interesting, although simultaneously far more general. We pass progressively from the erotogenic zone, as a privileged *place* for stimulation, to a far more extended series of processes. Already in the text of the *Three Essays*, but even more as Freud's considerations expand through broader clinical experience, the capacity to be the point of departure of sexual stimulation is revealed to be by no means the privilege of those zones which are successively described as the *loci* of oral, anal, urethral, or genital sexuality. Indeed, it is not exclusively those well-localized zones with their cutaneo-mucous covering, but every cutaneous region which is capable of serving as point of departure for sexual stimulation. In a later stage of his thought, Freud will posit that the erotogenic (areas productive of sexual stimulation) includes not simply every cutaneous region, but every organ, including internal ones; in so doing, he drew on an interpretation of the symptoms of hypochondria.[14] Then, generalizing still further, he is eventually led to the position that every function and, finally, every human activity can be erotogenic. We are drawing in this last observation on the chapter in the *Three Essays* dealing with "indirect sources" of sexuality in order to note this time that far from being simply a biochemical process *localizable* in an organ or in a collection of differentiated cells, the "source" of sexuality can be as general a process as the mechanical stimulation of the body in its entirety; take, for example, the rocking of an infant or the sexual stimulation that may result from rhythmic jolts, as in the course of a railroad trip; or the example of sexual stimulation linked to muscular activity, specifically to sports. Then, in a still vaster perspective, Freud comes to assert that intense intellectual effort can itself be a point of departure for sexual stimulation—a fact that the most ordinary clinical observation confirms. Such is also the case for such general processes as affects, notably "painful" affects; thus, a suddenly emergent state of anxiety will frequently trigger a sexual stimulation. We shall, moreover, in a subsequent discussion of masochism, have occasion to return to the painful affect as an "indirect source" of sexuality.

Freud's conclusion on the subject reads:

Sexual excitation arises as a concomitant effect [we shall retain this term *Nebenwirkung*, "marginal effect," for it defines the process of propping in its double movement of leaning, and then detachment or deviation] in the case of a great number of internal processes [mechanical stimulation, muscular activity, intellectual work, etc.] as soon as the intensity of those processes passes beyond certain quantitative limits. What we have called the component drives [*Partialtriebe, pulsions partielles*] of sexuality are either derived directly from these internal sources or are composed of elements both from those sources and from the erotogenic zones.[15]

We thus see the priority accorded by Freud, not to the source in its strictly physiological sense, but to the source in its so-called "indirect" sense, as in an "internal source" which ultimately is nothing but the transcription of the sexual repercussions of anything occurring in the body beyond a certain quantitative threshhold. The interest of this redefinition of the source lies in the fact that any function, any vital process, can "secrete" sexuality; any agitation may participate in it. Sexuality in its entirety is in the slight deviation, the *clinamen* from the function. It is in the *clinamen* insofar as the latter results in an autoerotic internalization.

What, then, is ultimately the source of the drive? In the present perspective, we may say that it is the *instinct* in its entirety. The entire instinct with its own "source," "impetus," "aim," and "object," as we have defined them; the instinct, kit and caboodle with its four factors, is in turn the source of a process which mimics, displaces, and denatures it: the drive. To that extent the erotogenic zone, the privileged somatic zone, is not quite a source in the same sense as one might speak of the somatic source of an instinct; it is, rather, defined as a point particularly exposed to the concomitant, or marginal, effect—the *Nebenwirkung*—we have just evoked.

We thus conclude an all too brief itinerary. We shall put aside a consideration of the third chapter of the *Three Essays* in favor of other topics, and characterize it simply as the moment of the instinct regained; regained, as in any rediscovery—we demonstrated as much above concerning the rediscovery of the object—as other than it was in the beginning, for the discovery is always a rediscovery of *something else*. Clearly, this phase is oedipal. We shall presently neglect this third stage in order to insist on what gives to the first two chapters their meaning, orientation, and unity. Consider once more what they entail: to that end we shall use the term *perversion*, since that indeed is the focus of the first chapter, with the sexual aberrations of adults, as well as of the second with the notion of a "polymorphous perverse" child. We shall consider the term *perversion* and the kind of movement operative within its very concept. Perversion? The notion is commonly defined as a *deviation from instinct*, which presupposes a specific path and aim and implies the choice of a divergent path (in biology, and currently in the "human sciences," reference is often made to "deviants"). This is so clearly the case that a glance at any psychiatric textbook reveals that its authors admit a remarkable diversity of perversions, concerning the entirety of the field of "instincts" and according to the number and classification of the instincts they adopt; not only sexual perversions but also, and perhaps above all, perversions of the moral sense, of the social instincts, of the nutritive instinct, etc. In the *Three Essays*, on the contrary, Freud founds his notion of perversion strictly on the sexual perversions. Are we thus suggesting, since deviance is necessarily defined in relation to a norm, that Freud himself would rally to the notion of a sexual instinct? Moreover, the definition of a "sexual instinct" ultimately would consist only in a revised and improved version of the "popular conception." Such is not the case, for Freud's dialectic is more fundamental. The movement we sketched above, a movement of exposition which is simultaneously the movement of a system of thought and, in the last analysis, the movement of the thing itself, is that the *exception*—i.e., the perversion—ends up by *taking the rule along with it*. The exception, which should presuppose the existence of a definite instinct, a preexistent sexual function, with its well-defined norms of accomplishment; that exception ends up by undermining and destroying the very notion of a biological norm. The whole of sexuality, or at least the whole of infantile sexuality, ends up by becoming perversion.

What, then, is perverted, since we may no longer refer to a "sexual instinct," at least in the case of the small child? What is perverted is still the instinct, but it is as a vital function that it is perverted *by* sexuality. Thus the two notions discussed at the beginning of this chapter—instinct and drive—once more are seen to meet and separate. The drive properly speaking, in the only sense faithful to Freud's discovery, *is* sexuality. Now sexuality, in its entirety, in the human infant, lies in *a movement which deflects the instinct, metaphorizes its aim, displaces and internalizes its object, and concentrates its source on what is ultimately a minimal zone, the erotogenic zone.* Concerning that erotogenic zone, which we have barely discussed, we should indicate the interest we are inclined to attribute to it. It is a kind of breaking or turning point within the bodily envelope, since what is in question is above all sphincteral orifices: mouth, anus, etc. It is also a zone of exchange, since the principal biological exchanges are borne by it (the prime example is again feeding, but there are other exchanges as well). This zone of exchange is also a zone for care, namely the particular and attentive care provided by the mother. These zones, then, attract the first erotogenic maneuvers from the adult. An even more significant factor, if we introduce the subjectivity of the first "partner": these zones *focalize parental fantasies* and above all *maternal fantasies*, so that we may say, in what is barely a metaphor, that they are the points through which is *introduced into the child that alien internal entity* which is, properly speaking, *the sexual excitation*. It is this alien internal entity and its evolution within the human being which will be the object of our next study.

2

Sexuality and the Vital Order in Psychical Conflict

In beginning this second elaboration, which is also concerned with sexuality, we shall first propose a series of observations relating to our previous lecture, which was no doubt too brief to trace a Freudian genesis of sexuality from the vital order. First of all, it should be noted that our earlier effort was a necessarily imperfect approximation. We only developed a single *aspect* of the problem of sexuality. The very term *genesis* evokes the notion of an emergence, the possibility of a linear understanding of what is later by what precedes it. But this perspective should be corrected by a reversal: on the one hand, the proposed genesis implies in fact that what comes first—say, the vital order—contains what might be called a fundamental imperfection in the human being: a dehiscence. What is "perverted" by sexuality is indeed the function, but a function which is somehow feeble or premature. Therein lies the whole problem of the "vital order" in man and of the possibility, or rather the impossibility, of grasping it "beneath" what has come to "cover" it over (assuming that these terms still have any other than a strictly didactic function). On the other hand, to that very extent, it is the *later* which is perhaps more important, and alone allows us to understand and to interpret what we persist in calling *the prior*. We are alluding here to a notion which is equally prevalent in Freud's thought, and which will presently figure between the lines of what we shall undertake to explain: the notion of "deferred action" (*Nachträglichkeit*).[1]

Our second preliminary observation, similarly undertaken along with Freud, bears on the extraordinary broadening of the notion of sexuality occasioned by psychoanalysis, a broadening as much in the extension of the concept as in its comprehension. In its *extension*, since sexuality would seem to include not only the small sector of genital activity, not only perversions or neuroses, but all of human activity, as the introduction of the concept of sublimation, for example, demonstrates. At this point we should recall the term *pansexuality* which was used as a veritable

25

war horse against Freud, a polemical arm against which he was often hard put to defend himself. He did, of course, come up with a defense, often aggressively, as though parrying a malevolent attack, but somehow always obliquely as well. Most often Freud pretended to understand "pansexuality" in the most pejorative and least defensible sense, taking literally the reproach of his least subtle adversaries: you explain everything only by sexuality. Thereupon he could easily respond that his theory entailed nothing of the sort, since it was based entirely on conflict and conflict implies duality. Something is always opposed to sexuality, even if that opposite term is defined differently in various stages of Freud's thought: it may be another kind of drive—what Freud terms self-preservative drives or ego drives—or it may be the ego, as a structure, itself; and in the last analysis, it will be the death drive. Freud is thus responding to an objection that he deliberately formulates in the most absurd manner: you explain everything only by sexuality; but in fact he does not answer—and for good reason—the objection: you put sexuality everywhere. For "pansexuality" does not necessarily mean that sexuality is "everything," but perhaps that *in "everything"* there is sexuality. "And for good reason" if it is indeed true, as we have attempted to demonstrate above, that *everything* can generate sexuality—which implies that everything in our clinical experience can lead back to it as well.

Ultimately, Freud's response to these "calumnies" consists, in fact, in a counterattack: your objection is only an index of your own repression. We shall quote here a passage which is striking in its modernity, above all if it is related to recent studies of the diffusion of psychoanalytic concepts in contemporary society. In his work on "psychoanalysis, its image, and its public," Moscovici, in fact, undertook to determine, through a broad series of questionnaires, just what the public currently understands by that term.[2] Moscovici discovered that psychoanalysis—not for specialists, of course, but for the man in the street—means quite simply "repression" and "sexuality." Now here is what Freud writes in his 1920 preface to the fourth edition of the *Three Essays*:

Now that the flood-waters of war have subsided, it is satisfactory to be able to record the fact that interest in psychoanalytic research remains unimpaired in the world at large. But the different parts of the theory have not all had the same history [which is what Moscovici demonstrated more scientifically]. The purely psychological theses and findings of psychoanalysis on the unconscious, repression, conflict as a cause of illness, the advantage accruing from illness, the mechanisms of the formations of symptoms, etc., have come to enjoy increasing recognition and have won notice even from those who are in general opposed to our views. [As far as psychoanalytic "psychology" was concerned, everyone was beginning to agree—and increasingly so—on accepting and naturalizing it.] That part of the theory, however, which lies on the frontiers of biology [by which we may understand: sexuality], and the foundations of which are contained in this little work is still faced with undiminished contradiction. It has even led some who for a time took a very active interest in psychoanalysis to abandon it and to adopt fresh views which were intended to restrict once more the part played by the factor of sexuality in normal and pathological mental life.[3]

We indicated earlier just what Moscovici's poll had revealed: for the "nonspecialist," sexuality is indeed the essential contribution of psychoanalysis to contemporary thought. Freud emphasizes, on the other hand, that for "scientists," sexuality is precisely what is relegated to the shadows, whereas what is more easily accepted and integrated are certain *mechanisms* described in psychoanalysis (e.g., repression, advantages accruing from illness, etc.). We might say, more schematically and polemically, that *what is accepted is repression but what is repressed is . . . the repressed; and the repressed is sexuality.*

We shall quote another passage in the same preface. Freud is responding here to the accusation of "pansexuality"; and we shall see that in a certain sense he by no means claims *not* to be a "pansexualist":

It must also be remembered, however, that some of what this book contains—its insistence upon the importance of sexuality in all human achievements and the attempt that it makes at enlarging the concept of sexuality—has from the first provided the strongest motives for the resistance against psychoanalysis. People have gone so far in their search for high-sounding catchwords as to talk of the "pan-sexualism" of psychoanalysis and to raise the senseless charge against it of explaining "everything" by sex. We might be astonished at this, if we ourselves could forget the way in which emotional factors make people confused and forgetful. For it is some time since Arthur Schopenhauer, the philosopher, showed mankind the extent to which their activities are determined by sexual impulses—in the ordinary sense of the word.[4]

We shall now approach the second question, no longer that of the extension (in the logical sense of the word) of sexuality to the entire domain of human activity, but that posed by the broadening *in comprehension*, and ultimately the change in meaning, undergone by the word *sexuality*. Here are the few words Freud devotes to the question in the same preface:

And as for the "stretching" of the concept of sexuality which has been necessitated by the analysis of children and what are called perverts, anyone who looks down with contempt upon psychoanalysis from a superior vantage-point should remember how closely the enlarged sexuality of psychoanalysis coincides with the Eros of the divine Plato.[5]

"Enlarged sexuality": such indeed has been our focus since we moved from the sexual as a vital instinct to the sexual as a veritable universal perversion of the instinctual (or, to use a term which, if not quite synonymous, belongs at least to the same register: a perversion of the functional). Throughout his work, Freud struggled with this problem and defended himself against the various objections addressed to him concerning it. In so doing, he needed a new definition of sexuality, since he came to realize that the old one—referring to genital sex with fixed aim and specific object—had proved unacceptable. His attention was briefly drawn to a phrase which was probably promoted by the sexologists who at times gravitated in the psychoanalytic orbit—*organ pleasure*—which serves to designate precisely that perversion of the instinctual referred to in opposition—we would hypothesize with due plausibility—to the idea of *functional pleasure*. Sexuality is indeed a localized, autoerotic pleasure, a pleasure of the organ "in place," in opposition to a functional pleasure with all which that term implies of an opening towards the object. Freud occasionally uses the phrase "organ pleasure" to the extent that it helps in understanding, but he is also distrustful of it, since the introduction of a "synonym" risks obliterating the affirmation that the whole of the process described is through and through sexual. To eliminate the very word *sexual* is, for him, to relinquish the idea: we know how punctilious Freud is about questions of words and see him more than once affirm that to yield the word is to surrender three-quarters of the very contents of his thought. It seems to us in any event that if the difficulty with which Freud struggled denotes a certain instability in his thought, it is a necessary instability which appears temporarily when, in the dialectical evolution of a science, a theory is overturned and replaced by a new theory whose generalized axiomatic allows for the inclusion of the earlier theory as a particular case. From the point of view of the subject, of the scientist, the scientific revolution which suddenly enlarges the meaning of a concept sweeps away, we might say, its very ground. Such is the case for Freud himself: at which point we see him taking refuge in the hopes for a biological, chemical, or hormonal definition of sexuality, a hope whose fulfillment is perpetually put off to some distant future of science; or we see him simply repeating, as though he could progress no further, the reasons which force him to *assimilate* the domain he discovered to sex in the popular, "genital" sense of the word. To recall the principal arguments: the *resemblance*, for instance, that can exist between pregenital pleasure and genital pleasure; the *contiguity*, the barely perceptible transitions linking a whole series of pleasures, the last of the series being frequently a genital pleasure or, in any event, one with a genital meaning. Take, for instance, all those not quite genital transitions in the child ending in masturbation; or, in the adult, what is called foreplay to the sexual act; or those perverse practices which can be quite extragenital but which nevertheless also lead to sexual excitation in the narrow sense of the word; or, finally, all those links found in neurotic symptoms between nonsexual pleasure and pleasure with a sexual meaning. Ultimately we are confronted with the argument *ad hominem* of repression, which is defiant of a certain logic, but irrefutable in psychoanalysis. Here is the form it takes in the present case: if "sensual sucking," an autoerotic manifestation, is condemned by mothers, it is clearly because they recognize implicitly that it is a "bad habit," and as is well known, "bad habit" is only a euphemism for a habit leading to sexual stimulation and enjoyment. In the case of mothers, we invariably find a double resistance: simultaneously against the *notion* of infantile sexuality and against its *manifestations*. Which is to say that they affirm simultaneously these two contradictory propositions; the child is sexually innocent, and since he isn't, he should be condemned. We recognize here a version of Freud's famous "kettle" argument: you never loaned me that kettle; moreover, it was broken, and anyway, I already returned it to you. On all fronts, sexuality, in the Freudian sense, leads to repression and denial. At stake is something which is obscurely and perhaps irremediably condemnable, even if today, in the post-Freudian era, the expression "infantile sexuality" seems far less frightening. In this regard, we shall quote the malicious remark of a child analyst whom we once asked the question: in your experience, what does "infantile sexuality," which we all talk about, finally mean? Her response was more or less as follows: it's a handy term adults use in order to mask a host of thoroughly frightening things they don't want to face up to.

Sexuality is thus the repressed *par excellence*, and from one end to the other, that affirmation will be found to recur in Freud's work. What may obscure that thesis and consequently motivate the illusions of an elaborate "psychologizing" tendency in our discipline is the fact that Freud on occasion gave a description of the mechanism of conflict—or of the *mechanism* of repression—in abstraction from its contents. We are referring specifically to a late text, the *Outline of Psychoanalysis* (1938), which, however informative it may be in other respects, describes in an initial stage—through an expository artifice that is not without serious drawbacks—psychical conflict as an abstract conflict between as yet unspecified agencies: on one side, the ego, on the other what is called the "id," the locus of drives, but without including in that "id" anything precise, without specifying a particular drive, notably sexuality. One has the impression from such descriptions, and even more so from those authors who undertake to explain Freud's metapsychology, that on the one hand there are psychological processes which can be adequately described in terms of mechanics, and that on the other hand, the abstract scheme of conflict can be fleshed out with any kind of "drive": sexuality in one case, aggressiveness in another, elsewhere, no doubt, a third type. A bit later in the *Outline of Psychoanalysis*,[6] however, Freud will return to the subject and explicitly ask the following question: even though the broad lines of conflict and the mechanism of repression can apparently be described in all their generality, how is it, *in fact*, that one's sexual life constitutes the only weak point on which repression electively comes to bear? Why is it our sexuality alone which is repressed? In those pages, several valuable indications are offered concerning certain specific characteristics of the human sexual drive, notably its "diphasic onset," the fact that it appears in two stages: on the one hand, an infantile phase; on the other, that of puberty and adulthood, the two being separated by a long period called the "latency period." At stake is a characteristic whose import is more important than the simple "maturational" factor which serves as its basis. The process invoked involves a temporal rhythm: a first, "premature" appearance of sexuality; an eclipse through repression; a reassumption of the earlier meanings on the basis of physiological possibilities now adequate to their intention. We shall shortly see how Freud brings this rhythmic factor into play in the phenomenon of repression. A further and no less interesting observation in the same passage emphasizes what may be called the denaturation of sexuality in humans in relation to animals: for example, the loss of the periodic character of sexual excitability which is specific to animal sexuality. Thus a natural, functional rhythm (that of rutting) disappears, while elsewhere there emerges a different kind of sequence, which is incomprehensible without calling into play such categories as repression, reminiscence, work of elaboration, "deferred action."

All these remarks in the *Outline* are suggestive, but relatively undeveloped and barely articulated into a coherent whole. Sexuality is indeed designated as the "weak point" in psychical organization, but the explanatory link between that "weakness" and the process of repression is not specified. It is as though this late text no longer presented anything but the muffled echo of a question which Freud had asked at the beginning, far more acutely, and which he formulated at the inception of his metapsychological inquiries in 1895 as follows: *"There must be some attribute of sexual ideas to explain why they alone are subject to repression."* That affirmation appears in the *Project for a Scientific Psychology* of 1895, a crucial text for our inquiry if it is indeed true that Freud's most elaborate attempt to relate internally repression and sexuality in a common theory dates from that period. We refer here to what might be labeled the "seduction theory" or the theory of the "hysterical *proton pseudos* [first lie]," a theory which constitutes the core not only of the entire second section of the *Project for a Scientific Psychology* but also of the larger part of Freud's theoretical writings from then on until 1900. The seduction theory? The theory of the *proton pseudos*? It is, of course, difficult to free certain notions from a kind of terminological slag, from a partially antiquated conceptual apparatus which makes access to the *Project* rather difficult. The uneasiness of the contemporary reader upon encountering this text is beyond question. Either he takes Freud's conceptualization literally, until, recovering his senses, he begins wondering whether he has not been swallowed up by some monstrous pseudo-scientific machine, with minimal relation to "psychological realities"; or he is tempted to distinguish at the outset what the text conveys of emergent psychoanalytic truth from the vestiges of a banally scientistic mode of thought; but if that second attitude is adopted, it must also be conceded that the larger part of the *Project* should be rejected. Yet, despite the opinion of numerous historians of Freud's thought,[7] despite the judgment of Freud himself,[8] we have systematically undertaken to enter into the complex labyrinth of the text, submitting to its "technicality" in all the offensiveness of its detail. We do so guided by the conviction that a great work—informed by a great experience—cannot be so easily dismembered into good and bad parts.

Without repeating presently—or even beginning—that long process, we shall nevertheless attempt to focus on the essential aspect of the notion of *seduction*. In Freud's thought, seduction may be situated in two different registers: on the one hand, it is a *clinical observation*, which is successively affirmed, refuted, called into question, and once again reaffirmed until and through Freud's final texts; on the other hand, it is a *theory* elaborated on the basis of that observation of the fact(s) of seduction.

The observation is initially quite simple. Through psychoanalysis, one discovers what appear at first sight to be memories—or at least scenes, whatever truth value one accords to them—in which an adult makes sexual advances towards a child, in either words or more or less explicit gestures, occasionally including even the beginnings—if not the conclusions—of specific sexual acts. In the *Studies on Hysteria* (published in 1895), which recounts most of the early cases of Freud and Breuer, the reference to seduction in hysterical memories is constant. In certain of these observations, the memories are retold in the form in which they were actually rediscovered; occasionally, they are partially distorted or censored by the author (as he himself will subsequently explain) when he is not yet prepared to face his discovery in all its scope—i.e., the discovery of the oedipus complex—and attributes to an "uncle" what in fact, we are told in a footnote, was the doing of a *father*. For the hysterics treated in that period through the "cathartic method," seduction was thus a common scenario, found over and over in a succession of scenes whose sequence Freud would enthusiastically retrace in tireless pursuit, beyond every "later" scene, of an earlier and more "traumatic" analogous event. This impassioned search for "scenes," for *the* scene, and ultimately for the primal scene, was fated to end in a dramatic experience of disillusionment, expressed in a letter (69) dated 21 September 1897 to Fliess. We shall now quote and comment upon several passages in that letter:

Here I am again—we returned yesterday morning—refreshed, cheerful, impoverished and without work for the time being, and I am writing to you as soon as we have settled in again. Let me tell you straightaway the great secret which has been slowly dawning on me in recent months. I no longer believe in my *neurotica* [more precisely, in the theory of neurosis based on seduction and the "proton pseudos"]. That is hardly intelligible without an explanation; you yourself found what I told you credible. So I shall start at the beginning and tell you the whole story of how the reasons for rejecting it arose. The first group of factors were the continual disappointment of my attempts to bring my analyses to a real conclusion, the running away of people who for a time had seemed my most favorably inclined patients, the lack of the complete success on which I had counted, and the possibility of explaining my partial successes in other, familiar ways. [Here Freud is simply summarizing, in a most general way, his therapeutic failures.] Then there was the astonishing thing that in every case . . . blame was laid on perverse acts by the father [indeed, if one were obliged to rediscover seduction scenes, one would also have to diagnose clinically the fathers of hysterics and admit that they must be sexual perverts to attack their children], and realization of the unexpected frequency of hysteria, in every case of which the same thing applied, though it was hardly credible that perverted acts against children were so general. (Perversion would have to be immeasurably more frequent than hysteria, as the illness can only arise where the events have accumulated and one of the factors which weaken defence is present.) [Here Freud is offering a statistical objection: the sexual perversion of parents would have to be infinitely more frequent than the hysteria of children since one would assume that there are more cases of seduction than those that result—in specifically determined circumstances—in hysterical neurosis.[9]] Thirdly, there was the definite realization that there is no "indication of reality" in the unconscious, so that it is impossible to distinguish between truth and emotionally-charged fiction [i.e., between truth and fantasy; here we encounter one of the cornerstones of Freudian theory: in the unconscious, there is no "indication of reality" allowing one to distinguish a "real" memory from pure and simple imagination]. Fourthly, there was the consideration that even in the most deep-reaching psychoses the unconscious memory does not break through, so that the secret of infantile experiences is not revealed even in the most confused states of delirium [thus even in those cases most apparently favorable to an investigation of the unconscious—psychoses—ultimately, an initial event never emerges].[10]

In summary, Freud proposes, in opposition to his own theory, objections of fact—the impossibility of ever rediscovering *the* "scene"—and of principle: the impossibility of admitting that paternal perversion is *that* frequent and, above all, the inability to decide whether a scene discovered in analysis is true or fantasied.

Freud's letter has generally been greeted as the negative moment announcing a major discovery and clearing away obstacles on the path to fantasy, that "royal road" of psychoanalysis, to paraphrase Freud's comment on dreams. And it is on the territory conquered through that discovery that we analysts continue to function, if it is indeed true that the core of psychoanalytic work consists in an explicitation and analysis of unconscious fantasy. The exploration of fantasy has proved, in fact, a remarkably fruitful path for us, but a remarkably painful one for Freud to the extent that, despite the introduction of the category of "psychical reality," on which he will insist increasingly, he found himself caught in an alternative which, in recent years, we have attempted to go beyond: that between the real, on the one hand, the reality of a lived memory whose trace can be detected in an almost sleuthlike manner,[11] and, on the other hand, the imaginary, traditionally conceived of as a lesser entity. We might say that he failed to render explicit what is, nevertheless, present in the notion of "psychical reality," something which would have all the consistency of the real without, however, being verifiable in external experience, a category which might, on first approach, be designated as the "structural."

Starting with this historic juncture in 1897, throughout the whole of Freud's work, an endless series of oscillations concerning seduction and, more generally, the reality of primal sexual scenes may be discovered. We will not retrace the history of those variations,[12] whose very existence demonstrates that Freud by no means achieved a *definitive* mastery of the category of "psychical reality"; thus, even though he affirms that, after all, it makes little difference whether what has been discovered is reality or fantasy, since fantasy has its own reality, he is continually in search of factual clues concerning what happened in childhood. We shall simply recall that the principal point of reference here is the analysis of the "Wolf Man" and the discussion, to which numerous pages in the case history are devoted, of whether the "primal scene"—the witnessing of parental intercourse—was in fact observed by the patient or simply refabricated from later events or virtually insignificant clues.

Nevertheless, despite the incessant oscillation between such terms as *reality, pure imagination, retrospective reconstruction,* etc., Freud will reaffirm with increasing insistence the *fact* of seduction, going so far as to present it, at the conclusion of his work (in the *New Introductory Lectures*) as a quasi-universal datum: for there is indeed a form of seduction which practically no human being escapes, the seduction of maternal care. The first gestures of a mother towards her child are necessarily impregnated with sexuality, an observation which overlaps with our earlier formulation concerning the polarization of infantile sexuality in the "erotogenic zones."[13]

Having considered seduction as a *scene*, we now turn to the *theory* of seduction. *Proton pseudos*: a first—specifically: hysterical—lie. Hysterics tend to lie, as is known and as was by no means unknown before Freud. We only just now reobserved that fact with Freud, since they propose as a scene allegedly belonging to their childhood something we are eventually obliged to consider as entirely imaginary. They have taken their imagination for reality, and more fundamentally, they have translated—according to specific laws of transposition—their desire into reality: in the present case, in what is called a "primal fantasy" of seduction, their own desire to seduce the father has been translated, in inverse form, into an actual scene of seduction *by* the father. With the term *proton pseudos*, however, something other than a subjective lie is being invoked; at stake is a transition from the subjective to a grounding—perhaps even to a transcendental—dimension: in any event a kind of objective lie inscribed in the facts. From its inception, definitively, psychoanalysis thus maintained itself beyond the banalities of official "clinical" practice, which regularly invoked bad faith and simulation to account for what it called "pithiatism." If hysterics lie, they are above all the first victims of a kind of lie or deception. Not that they have been lied to; it is rather as though there existed in the facts themselves a kind of fundamental duplicity for which we would propose the term *deceit* [*fallace*]. "Primal deceit": perhaps such is our best translation of the *proton pseudos* in its specificity.

The theory of seduction or of a "primal deceit" is a theory of repression and, consequently, of a major category of defense. And in the *Project for a Scientific Psychology*, which undertakes to construct a *psychology*, the problem is posed in the more general framework of a psychology of defense. Freud will generate the specificity of repression through a comparison with normal modes of defense. For psychological observation does, in fact, allow us to describe numerous cases—e.g., defense against painful memories or perceptions—in which clearly definable, normal psychological mechanisms are employed. Those mechanisms call into play a variety of factors: ego attention; a gradual attenuation through repetition and discharge by degrees; the establishment of associative connections permitting a linking of an excessively "charged" memory to other memories and ideas, thus englobing it in a mental flux in which its charge is progressively distributed and diluted. This last factor constitutes what Freud calls "elaboration," a process which remains, under the names of "elaboration" or "working through," one of the mainsprings of psychoanalytic therapy: causing the readmission into the current of mental life of something which, up until then, had remained isolated and encysted. Now, if this mechanism of elaboration is employed in the normal manner, it happens that in certain cases the subject is deprived of any recourse to it. But first, we shall quote one of any number of passages in which Freud describes the "normal" mechanism of defense:

There are, however, other occasions on which memories release unpleasure; and in the case of recent memories this is quite normally so. If a trauma (an experience of pain) occurs for the first time when there is already an ego in existence [this is the important point: when the ego is there *at the very beginning of the process*, the defense generally occurs in the "normal" manner]—the very first traumas of all escape the ego entirely—there is a release of unpleasure; but the ego is simultaneously at work creating lateral cathexes [this is an inhibiting process which prevents uncontrolled discharge from occurring].[14] If there is afterwards a cathexis of the *memory-trace* [i.e., if the painful memory is reactivated], the unpleasure is repeated; but the ego-facilitations are already present [the ego, more simply, is already accustomed], and experience shows that the second release of unpleasure is less—until, after further repetition, it is reduced to no more than a signal of an intensity acceptable to the ego [the crux is thus that starting with the first release of unpleasure, a process goes into effect resulting in a gradual attenuation]. Thus the essential thing is that there should be an inhibition by the ego on the occasion of the *first* release of unpleasure, so that the process does not occur as a "posthumous" primary affective experience [the meaning of the word "posthumous" will shortly become clear].[15]

We could reproduce numerous other passages, each corresponding to a further attempt—for Freud, in the *Project*, proceeds by successive approximations, without any pretense at a finished treatise—to explain the workings of "normal defense" by the "ego."

But the second chapter, devoted to psychopathology, is concerned, not with normal defense, but *hysterical defense*. In the case of the hysteric, the possibility of a normal defense through attenuation is not available; the memory is deprived of any elaboration; there is no associative network linking it (to take Freud's affirmations literally) to the rest of psychical life. A more precise grasp of Freud's logic here entails consideration of two different terms: on the one hand, the repressed scene, an unpleasant memory; on the other, an apparently subordinate, concomitant memory, a circumstance contingent to the traumatic event, which unlike that event, has remained in memory as a symptom or "symbol" of the first scene, which itself cannot be brought to consciousness. The connection between the two cannot be consciously maintained, as though, to phrase it in terms of hydraulics or "psychical economy," the entire "charge" passed constantly from one to the other, or as though the unconscious memory could not retain a sufficient charge, but transmitted directly and "fully," without any restriction or mediation, the whole of its affect to the conscious memory. Thus, in the *Studies on Hysteria*, Katharina, a patient, sees during her seizures of anxiety a face which she is absolutely incapable of associating with anything at all: a face entirely without meaning, but which becomes the focus of her anxiety. At the same time, the scene which initially provoked that anxiety, and in the course of which the face had been seen (but in an entirely extrinsic way), remains inaccessible. Every new perception which irritates the unconscious memory of the traumatizing event, and every new trauma which may echo it, results in the emergence into consciousness not of the scene itself but of the symbol of the scene, and of the symbol alone. Freud proposes a schematic version of the process, designating as *A* and *B*, respectively, the external circumstance and the scene which, in fact, motivated the repression:

A is an excessively intense idea, which forces its way into consciousness too often, and each time it does so leads to tears. [In the case in *Studies on Hysteria* just referred to the symptom consisted in an anxiety attack. In that example, *A* would be the face which appears, like a veritable hallucination, to Katharina and is linked with the anxiety.] The subject does not know why *A* makes him weep and regards it as absurd; but he cannot prevent it.[16]

That description refers to the condition before analysis, when the symptom exists. We shall now examine the situation after analysis:

It has been discovered that there is an idea *B* [say, a scene] which rightly leads to tears and which rightly recurs often until a certain complicated piece of psychical work directed against it has been completed by the subject. [As just indicated, that psychical work is a labor of connecting. That, essentially, is how the work of analysis was considered at that time. Thus scene *B*, which in fact justified the tears, is rediscovered by analysis and reworked until it is no longer in a position to be harmful.] The effect of *B* is not absurd, is comprehensible by the subject and can even be fought against by him.

B [say, the principal scene] stands in a particular relation to *A* [the mnemic symbol]. For there has been an event which consisted of *B* + *A*. *A* was a subsidiary circumstance, while *B* was well calculated to produce a lasting effect. The production of this event in memory now occurs as though *A* had taken *B*'s place. *A* has become a substitute, a "symbol" for *B*. Hence the incongruity; for *A* is accompanied by consequences which it does not seem to deserve, which are not appropriate to it.[17]

In summary, we are faced with the repression of a specific memory, in place of which a symptom emerges, which is in effect conceived of as the symbol of that repressed memory, a symbol which is quite extrinsic and ultimately quite subsidiary in relation to the memory. But at this point, Freud goes further and poses the problem again in relation to normal functioning:

Symbols are formed in this way normally as well. A soldier will sacrifice himself for a piece of coloured cloth on a pole [i.e., something quite extraneous: a flag], because it has become the symbol of his native country; and no one considers this neurotic. . . . The knight who fights for a lady's glove *knows*, in the first place, that the glove owes its importance to the lady; and, secondly, his worship of the glove does not in the least prevent him from thinking of the lady and serving her in other ways.[18]

Thus, in these two examples of "normal" symbols, what differentiates their case from that of hysteria is that here the memory of what is symbolized remains present or cathected; otherwise we would find ourselves faced with the following (and by no means unimaginable!) absurdity: a soldier capable of dying for a flag, or a knightly servant sacrificing himself for a glove, while forgetting completely the nation or lady behind the symbols: "The hysteric who is reduced to tears by A is unaware that this is because of the association A-B, and B itself plays no part whatever in his mental life. In this case the symbol has taken the place of the thing completely."[19]

It may, of course, be claimed that Freud's logic is in an "associationist" framework, but it should be noted that the way in which these "associations" work is quite peculiar: in the case under consideration, the symbolized term has evacuated its entire charge, the whole of the affect it provokes, into what symbolizes it. In invoking the term "evacuate," we are only taking up an expression with economic connotations used by Freud in the passage immediately following. We are thus able to focus on one of those moments in which economic concepts emerge directly from clinical practice; those concepts are but the immediate transcription for Freud of what he observes of the play between affect and ideational representative. Here now is the explanation of the phenomenon from an economic point of view:

The term "excessively intense" points to *quantitative* characteristics. It is plausible to suppose that repression has the quantitative sense of being denuded of quantity, and that the sum of the two [i.e., the cathexis of the symbol plus the cathexis of the repressed] is equal to the normal. [This means that there is always the same quantity of affect, the same quantity of anxiety, or, we might say, the same "quantity of tears" in each case, and that the sum of $A + B$ will always produce the same affect. But what has been observed and is in need of explanation is that it is occasionally one, occasionally the other, or sometimes a distribution between the two, which provokes the affect.] If so, only the *distribution* of quantity has been altered. Something has been added to A that has been subtracted from B [B has been entirely emptied of all psychical energy, or in more technical terms, it has been decathected.] The pathological process is one of *displacement*, such as we have come to know in dreams, and is hence a primary process.[20]

Although we have followed Freud in his example of hysteria, we might indeed have sought support for his argument in the symbol in *dreams*. Exactly like the hysteric, a dreaming subject is capable of experiencing anxiety, desire, or pain when confronted with an idea which does not seem capable of motivating them. We discover, through dream analysis, that behind these ideas there are other "latent," completely "emptied" ones, which are entirely absent from the dream, so that the present idea, the manifest content or dream symbol, seems alone to be the cause of a totally absurd and irrational affect. Such is the model of what Freud calls the "primary process": specifically, *a total displacement of affect*, a complete communication, resulting in an idea, which is linked to a second one, retaining none of the psychical interest pertaining to it, but transmitting the whole of that psychical interest to the second one.

The primary process was discovered above all in phenomena of desire or wishes. Its "laws" are most easily demonstrated at the level of dreams considered as realizations of wishes. Now, in the case of repression, we encounter *a primary process which governs not so much the wish as the defensive mechanism*. A defense is a process invoked by the "ego," the agency whose function is precisely to moderate that frenetic circulation of affect in which the primary process consists, to arrange, for example, that when I say that *A equals B*, I retain simultaneously something of *A* without passing totally into *B*. How is it then that a mechanism directly dependent on the ego can at the same time be governed by the primary process? How is a pathological defense, functioning ultimately according to the laws of desire, possible? With that question, we come to the crux of the problem; and the following step in its resolution consists in demonstrating that *a pathological defense of such an order occurs only when it bears on a memory which is sexual in nature*.

The "scene"—and we shall soon see how—must necessarily come into contact with the domain of sexuality. Moreover, two scenes, rather than a single one, will be found to be necessary; and it is in their hiatus, and in what one is inclined to call the impressive bit of deceptive trickery that they give rise to, that the objective lie we have translated as "deceit" is generated. In his demonstration, Freud recounts quite briefly the case of a patient whom he does not speak of elsewhere, and to whom he gives the name Emma. Emma is a phobic whose symptom, in its remarkable simplicity, is a fear of entering stores by herself. Freud brings to light two scenes (since it is always scenes—scenarios or perceived tableaus—which are in question) in the case of this hysteric. He describes them in the order of their discovery, which is the regressive order of analysis: first, a conscious scene, dating from age twelve to thirteen; then, a scene which is rediscovered only through analysis, an earlier scene which may be situated at age eight. Contrary to Freud, we shall consider them in chronological order.

In speaking of the "first scene," we are well aware, of course, that Freud and other psychoanalysts after him were hardly satisfied with memories that may be regarded as extremely late. But of far greater import for us in this context than the age at which the scenes are dated is their *sequential scheme*. The "earlier" scene, then, the one that had been repressed and that analysis succeeded in bringing to light, has as its protagonist a merchant running a grocery store, who perpetrates on little Emma what Freud calls a "sexual assault":

On two occasions, when she was a child of eight, she had gone into a shop to buy some sweets and the shopkeeper had grabbed at her genitals through her clothes. In spite of the first experience she had gone to the shop a second time, after which she had stayed away. Afterwards she reproached herself for having gone the second time, as though she had wanted to provoke the assault. And in fact a "bad conscience" by which she was oppressed could be traced back to this experience.[21]

For the moment, we shall insist on only two points: the *repetitive* nature of the scene, and the *inverted* interpretation which might be proposed, and which we will subsequently not fail to give: there has undoubtedly been a sexual assault by the adult but it might also be said that, inversely, there has been seduction by the little girl, since she returns to the store, clearly in order to submit again to the same kind of act. To the extent that memory and fantasy can condense into a single scene several successive events as well as *distribute* into a temporal sequence the simultaneous elements of an experience, nothing prevents us from wondering whether the girl, *on the very first occasion*, had not gone into the store, moved by some obscure sexual premonition. The separation, isolation, and cleavage in the memory would function to free the subject from guilt.

The *second scene*, for its part, seems to contain no sexual incident, and the patient recounted it at the beginning of her analysis, attributing to it the origin of her phobia: "She explained it by a memory dating from the age of twelve (shortly after her puberty).[22] She went into a shop to buy something, saw the two shop assistants (one of whom she remembers) laughing together and rushed out in some kind of *fright*."[23] Thus: two shop assistants who are perhaps laughing at her, she thinks, because of the way she is dressed. We shall indicate without further delay the result of the dialectic generated between the two scenes: the first, containing a sexual meaning, will be repressed, and in conformity with the scheme in which term *B* is replaced by term *A*, we will find the symptom or mnemic symbol in its place: a phobia concerning stores. Between those two scenes, Freud elaborates an entire network of connections, summarized in a graphic diagram of the kind that might be established for a dream. He indicates precisely the associative links between the elements of the conscious scene and those of the previously unconscious one, associative links which themselves appear to be quite extraneous, harmless, and, in any event, nonsexual: on the one hand, clothing and, on the other, laughter, the laughter of two shop assistants which finds its equivalent or counterpart in the shopkeeper's grimace in the first scene. Thus: two scenes linked by associative chains, but also clearly separated from each other by a *temporal barrier which inscribes them in two different spheres of meaning: the moment of puberty.* And in the theory of the "proton pseudos" *that* is the crucial factor: between the two scenes an entirely new element has appeared—the possibility of a sexual reaction. When we speak of a "sexual reaction," moreover, we are evoking not only the possibility of new physiological reactions, but, in correlation, the existence of sexual ideas. In other words, at the time of the first scene, Emma is incapable of linking what happened to anything *corresponding* to it within her. On the contrary, in the second scene, she has ideas allowing her to understand what a sexual assault is.

This intervention of puberty introduces a curious inversion between the two scenes. It may be said, and these are virtually the terms of Freud himself, that in the first scene we have a sexual content in the explicit behavior of the adult protagonist, but that it is a sexual content, as it were, *in itself* and not *for the subject*. The scene is sexual for an outside spectator or in the intention of the shopkeeper. For the child it cannot have fully that meaning. A scene, then, which has no immediate sexual effect, produces no excitation, and provokes no defense; and the term Freud uses to characterize it effectively conveys this ambiguous or even contradictory quality: the scene is said to be "sexual-presexual." Of the second scene, on the other hand, we might also say that it is equally lacking in sexuality, since it involves apparently banal circumstances, the fact that two shop assistants laugh at an adolescent's clothing. No doubt, we might expand on the underlying sexual atmosphere of the scenario (convulsive laughter, flight, etc.). What is beyond question is that there is no sexual assault. Now that scene, however it may, in fact, have transpired, will reactivate the memory of the first scene, and through the mediation of that memory, "trigger" or "release" (*entbinden*) a sexual reaction in its double form: both a physiological excitation and a series of ideas that young Emma, now in puberty, will henceforth have at her disposition.

Here now is how Freud synthesizes the relation between the two scenes and how he arrives at the conclusion that the memory of the first scene, at the moment that the second scene occurs, cannot be the object of a "normal" defense (a defense by connection and attenuation) but must undergo an atypical or pathological defense:

It may be said to be quite usual for an association to pass through a number of unconscious intermediate links before arriving at a conscious one, as happened in this case. The element that enters consciousness is probably the one that arouses special interest. But in our example the remarkable thing is that what entered consciousness was not the element that aroused interest (the assault) but another which symbolized it (the clothes). [Thus the first scene does not penetrate into consciousness with its full meaning of assault but does so through an entirely extraneous element: the clothes.] If we ask what the cause of this interpolated pathological process may have been, we can only point to a single one—the sexual release, of which there was also evidence in consciousness. This was linked to the memory of the assault; but it is a highly noteworthy fact that it was not linked to the assault when it was actually experienced. [The first scene had no effect as provocation.] Here we have an instance of a memory exciting an affect which it had not excited as an experience, because in the meantime the changes produced by puberty had made possible a new understanding of what was remembered. Now this case is typical of repression in hysteria. We invariably find that a memory is repressed which has only become a trauma *after the event* [here is the heart of the argument: we try to track down the trauma, but the traumatic memory was only secondarily traumatic: we never manage to fix the traumatic event historically. This fact might be illustrated by the image of a Heisenberg-like "relation of indeterminacy": in situating the trauma, one cannot appreciate its traumatic impact, and *vice versa*.] The reason for this state of things is the retardation of puberty as compared with the remainder of the individual's development.[24]

"Trauma" is a notion in whose orbit Freud's thinking gravitated during the period of the *Project*, ever since his collaboration with Breuer and already during the years when he underwent the influence of Charcot. To reduce hysteria to a trauma was indeed the problem. But the model of the physical trauma, as an effraction or breach of external origin, is quite insufficient in the case of a psychical trauma. Here, an explanation can be achieved only through a scheme entailing two phases: it may be said that, in a sense, the trauma is situated entirely in the play of "deceit" producing a kind of seesaw effect between the two events. Neither of the two events in itself is traumatic; neither is a rush of excitation. The first one? It triggers nothing: neither excitation or reaction, nor symbolization or psychical elaboration; we saw why: the child, at the time she is the object of an adult assault, would not yet possess the ideas necessary to comprehend it. In that case, we may legitimately ask what the psychical status of the memory of the first scene is during the temporal interval separating it from the second one. It would seem that for Freud it persists neither in a conscious state nor, properly speaking, in a repressed state; it remains there, waiting in a kind of limbo, in a corner of the "preconscious"; the crucial point is that it is not linked to the rest of psychical life. We are thus confronted with the formation of what is called in the *Studies on Hysteria* a "separate psychical grouping."

If the first event is not traumatic, the second is, if possible, even less so. What is involved here is a nonsexual event, a banal scene out of daily life: going into a shop in which there are two assistants, perhaps convulsed with laughter. And yet it is that second scene which releases the excitation by awakening the memory of the first one: that memory acts from then on like a veritable "internal alien entity," henceforth attacking the subject from within, provoking within her sexual excitation.

To prove that this explanation is not bound to a passing phase of Freud's theory, we might invoke a whole series of passages and even the entirety of the texts dating from that period. We shall quote only a fragment from the *Studies on Hysteria*, which takes up the same idea, but is intelligible only in the context of the developments in the letters to Fliess and the *Project for a Scientific Psychology*:

> But the causal relation between the determining psychical trauma and the hysterical phenomenon is not of a kind implying that the trauma merely acts like an *agent provocateur* in releasing the symptom, which thereafter leads an independent existence. [The event, then, does not trigger the symptom which would persist by itself. We shall see that what persists is not the symptom, or rather that the symptom persists only because something else persists.] We must presume rather that the psychical trauma—or more precisely the memory of the trauma [what is traumatic, properly speaking, is not the event which we incorrectly call the psychical trauma, but the memory]—acts like a foreign body which long after its entry must be continued to be regarded as an agent that is still at work.[25]

From the model of physical trauma we have moved to psychical trauma; not through any vague or unthematized analogy from one domain to the other, but through a precise transition: the movement from the external to the internal. What defines psychical trauma is not any general quality of the psyche, but the fact that the psychical trauma comes from within. A kind of *internal-external* instance had been formed: a "spine in the flesh" or, we might say, a veritable spine in the *protective wall of the ego*. The early formulation of Freud and Breuer, in its apparent banality, means exactly the same thing: "hysterics suffer from reminiscences"; for the reminiscences are there like an internal object constantly attacking the ego. The reminiscence—or the fantasy—in the example of Emma is the internalization of the first "scene." Thus preserved from all attrition by the process of repression, the fantasy becomes a permanent source of free excitation. In this detour through the introjected, fantasied scene, we rediscover the notion of the *source* of the drive that we commented on in the preceding chapter from another point of view, based on the "biological" considerations present in the *Three Essays on the Theory of Sexuality*. Everything comes from without in

Freudian theory, it might be maintained, but at the same time every effect—in its efficacy—comes from within, from an isolated and encysted interior.

Finally, we shall quote the conclusion of the chapter on the "proton pseudos," in which once again normal defense is opposed to that quasi-impossibility of defense, or to that cataclysmic defense constituted by hysterical repression:

Thus it is the business of the ego to permit no release of affect, since this would at the same time permit a primary process. Its best instrument for this purpose is the mechanism of attention. If a cathexis which releases unpleasure were able to escape attention, the ego's intervention would come too late. And this is precisely what happens in the case of the hysterical *proton pseudos*. [The crux of the explanation will be the ego's inability to call into play the normal mechanisms of attention—this, to the very extent that the ego is "attacked," so to speak, on the side where it "least expected it." Its defenses are oriented in the direction of perception. Here, they will be taken from behind. Subsequently, we shall have to account for this "anthropomorphic" and apparently naïve terminology.] Attention is focused on perceptions, which are the normal occasions for the release of unpleasure. But here it is not a perception but a memory-trace which unexpectedly releases unpleasure, and the ego discovers this too late. It has permitted a primary process, because it did not expect one. . . . This confirms the importance of one of the preconditions that were indicated by clinical experience: *the retardation of puberty makes possible the occurrence of posthumous primary processes.*[26]

This entire passage may, in a sense, seem quite "historic" and consequently anachronistic in relation to what we now know—or believe we know—in psychoanalysis about the psychology of drives and, above all, about ego psychology. Which is why we shall raise, in a manner of concluding, a certain number of questions tending to bring into relief the essentially contemporary import of this segment of Freudian theory.

A first question: *Why sexuality?* Freud's answer is that sexuality alone is available for that action in two phases which is also an action "after the event." It is there and there alone that we find that complex and endlessly repeated interplay—midst a temporal succession of missed occasions—of "too early" and "too late." Fundamentally, what is at stake is the relation in the human being between his "acculturation" and his "biological" sexuality, on the condition that it be understood that the latter is already, for its part, partially "denatured." What exactly is too late? Biological sexuality with its maturational stages and above all the moment of puberty; such organic sexuality comes too late, failing to furnish the child (who constitutes the principal subject of the *Three Essays*) with "affective" and "ideational" counterparts sufficient to allow him to assimilate the sexual scene and to "understand" it. But at the same time sexuality comes too early as an interhuman relation; it comes from without, imported from the world of adults.

A second question may be grafted onto the first at this juncture: If the core of the Freudian scheme refers to this dialectic of the excessive earliness or lateness of puberty, and ultimately of the rhythm through which sexuality is established in man, might not the value of the explanation extend beyond the factual problem posed by the *circumstantial reality of seduction*? We recalled above, concerning seduction as a scene rather than as a theory, that Freud, up until the end of his work, continued to assert the reality of seduction scenes. He frequently returned to the subject, not without shifting the accent of his affirmations: finally, beyond any seduction scenes by the father, and beyond any openly genital seductions, he refers to seduction through maternal care as his *primary model*. Such care, in focusing on certain bodily regions, contributes to *defining* them as erotogenic zones, zones of exchange which demand and provoke excitation in order subsequently to reproduce it autonomously, through *internal* stimulation.

It is thus through excitation by means of maternal care that we can imagine the original form taken by seduction. But here, we should go a step further and not restrict ourselves to the pure materiality of stimulating actions, if indeed such "materiality" can ever be conceived of in isolation. We should, in fact, consider that beyond the contingency and transiency of any specific experience, it is the intrusion into the universe of the child of certain meanings of the adult world which is conveyed by the most ordinary and innocent of acts. The whole of the primal intersubjective relation—between mother and child—is saturated with these meanings. Such, we maintain, is the most profound sense of the theory of seduction and, above all, the sense which Freud ultimately gave to the very notion of seduction:

A child's intercourse with anyone responsible for his care affords him an unending source of sexual excitation and satisfaction from his erotogenic zones. This is especially so since the person in charge of him, who, after all, is as a rule his mother, herself regards him with feelings that are derived from her own sexual life: she strokes him, kisses him, rocks him and quite clearly treats him as a substitute for a complete sexual object.[27]

We should emphasize, moreover, that an interest in seduction was not limited to Freud alone: the notion was taken up by various disciples, notably by one of the most penetrating among them. Ferenczi, in his article "The Confusion of Tongues between Adults and the Child," presents the same idea in the form of a major opposition between a universe of the child—characterized by what the author calls "tenderness" —and an adult universe in which "passion" would reign.[28] By passion,

Ferenczi means sexuality, not only in its specifically aggressive dimension, but also in the "negativity" which seems intrinsic to it: the negativity of sexual enjoyment, reaching a peak in the annihilation of orgasm, the negativity of prohibitions: as to what not to do and above all what not to say. For Ferenczi the languages of tenderness and passion have their initial encounter in childhood, and it is that clash which is at the origin of trauma, of the first psychical conflict.

We should accustom ourselves to the idea that the meanings implicit in the slightest parental gesture bear the parents' fantasies; for it is, in fact, too often forgotten when we speak of the mother-child relation or of the parent-child relation that the parents themselves had their own parents; they have their "complexes," wishes marked by historicity, so that to reconstruct the child's oedipal complex as a triangular situation, while forgetting that at two vertices of the triangle each adult protagonist is himself the bearer of a small triangle and even of a whole series of interlocking triangles, is to neglect an essential aspect of the situation. In the final analysis the complete oedipal structure is *present from the beginning*, both "in itself" (in the objectivity of the familial configuration) but above all "in the other," outside the child. The path through which that entity "in itself" is appropriated passes initially through a confused and, in a sense, monstrous apprehension of the complex in a primordial other (theoretically, the mother).

Among the most original of Freud's followers—and among those most open to the discovery of the unconscious—Melanie Klein, after Ferenczi, deserves mention in this context. The "extravagance" of her theories and the obstinacy with which she is reproached for them are well known. She would introduce into the chronology of libidinal stages established by Freud an unheard-of reversal. Freud teaches, schematically, that the child's sexual activity is first oral, then anal, then phallic, and that it is in relation to phallic sexuality, towards age four or five, that what is called the oedipal complex, the problematic of castration, and finally genitality begin to appear. So much so that for certain psychoanalysts, whose consideration of matters may be a bit hasty, "oedipal" and "genital" are occasionally given as synonyms. Similarly, the "preoedipal"—i.e., the relations preceding the triangular structure child-mother-father—is often taken to be cognate with the "pregenital": occurring in the register of the elementary and nongenital sexual activities of orality and anality. Now Melanie Klein would introduce into this scheme total conceptual and chronological disorder: she speaks, for example, of an oral incorporation of the penis, locates in the first year a "precocious" oedipal complex, and thinks that the father, or at least his penis, plays a role for the child at the age of several months. Every one of Melanie Klein's propositions and interpretations plays havoc with our accepted ideas: not only with our

Freudian dogmas, but with our "common sense" (whose deceptiveness Freud, all the same, had already amply demonstrated); how can an infant of six months or a year fear, for example, an intrusion into his body of the paternal penis, an intrusion, moreover, apt to entail the most horrendous consequences (burns, laceration, devouring from within, fragmentation, etc.)? To what might such processes or fantasies—which very little in *direct* observation of the child corroborates—correspond? Indeed, the crudity or naïveté informing the expression of the most absurd scenarios may appear shocking, above all if not considered in relation with a *practice of interpretation* in child analysis. But even without the perspec- tive afforded by considerations of relation to practice, we are convinced that there exists a theoretical truth to Kleinian thought, a way of reinterpreting it so as to rediscover what, in "psychical reality," consti- tutes its basis. And that is precisely the fact that, starting with the first relations—even if they are "dual," with the mother alone, and the father absent (and indeed he is almost totally absent for the nursing infant)—a certain presence of a third element begins to play a role. In this sense, the father is present from the beginning, even if the mother is a widow: he is present because the mother herself has a father and desires a penis; and also, as we know, because the mother has libidinal designs on her own child and, *beyond* him, on the penis she desires. These truths—which are verified daily in the psychoanalysis of women, but which are all too easily forgotten when the children of these same women are in question—Klei- nian theory, through its fantasmatic detour, has recalled to our attention.

What is described schematically and in almost caricatural fashion as an *event* in the Freudian theory of the *proton pseudos* should be understood as a kind of implantation of adult sexuality in the child. We believe that it should be reinterpreted, not as an event, or as a datable lived trauma, but as a factor which is both more diffuse and more structural, a more primal factor as well in the sense that it is so linked to the process of humaniza- tion that it is only through abstraction that we can suppose the existence of a small human "before" that seduction. For, to be sure, to speak of a child who was initially "innocent" would be to forge a myth exactly symmetrical to the myth of seduction. Which brings us to a *third remark*.

At the beginning of this second chapter, we undertook to consider a theme that we have, no doubt, been able to treat only partially: sexuality and the vital order in psychical conflict. We have kept our promise in the sense that we did indeed pose the question, with Freud and following him, of how it is that sexuality should be found at the center of psychical conflict. But what is the factor—or the "force"—that enters into conflict with sexuality? At this point we encounter a whole series of possible answers, but initially we shall cite only two. A first solution: if it is true that we are indeed in the presence of an irruption of human sexuality into the vital order, if "life" is what sexuality comes to disturb, would it not be the entirety of those forces protecting that life—assembled under the rubric "instinct of self-preservation"—which would become the motor of repression? As we just indicated, however, it is doubtful that we have the right to hypostatize that vital order in the human being as an "earlier" state: an *a priori* or infrastructure. All that we know of the elementary vital mechanisms in the newborn infant, when compared with what happens in animals and even in small animals, demonstrates, on the contrary, the profoundly immature character of these vital functions in the human being; it is precisely by virtue of that factor that sexuality is introduced.

A second answer is offered by Freud from the very beginning of his work: what is opposed to sexuality and attacked by it "from within" is the "ego." We have seen that the meaning of *pseudos*—lie or fallacy—is *also* that the ego is outmaneuvered, taken from behind as by some ruse of war. The *proton pseudos* is also that ruse: the ego is taken from the side on which it "didn't expect it"; it is overcome, disarmed, subjected to the drive process, that primary process against which, however, it was in its entirety, *constituted*.

Thus our reflections on conflict and our interrogation of the forces opposed to sexuality bring us to the theme of our next two chapters: the problematics of the ego.

3

The Ego and the Vital Order

We shall first situate our argument by recalling the results of our first two studies: sexuality breaks out, in the human child, through *deviation from* and *autoerotic reversal of* the vital processes. And, on the other hand, sexuality—the term still taken in its "generalized" sense—appears as *implanted* in the child from the parental universe: from its structures, meanings, and fantasies.

Clearly, these are two sides of a single process: the autoerotic internalization and constitution of the "alien internal entity" (the fantasy), the perpetual source of the sexual drive. But, in another light, the second perspective had the effect of profoundly correcting the first. The genesis, in the first case, would still mean an emergence, a linear process, or, so to speak, a kind of secretion of sexuality by all the vital processes, all of which would imply, in a stage *prior* to autoerotism, the coherent existence of a vital order in man. The second perspective, on the contrary, allows us to conceive of phenomena only insofar as they are subject to the effect of "deferment" [*Nachträglichkeit, après coup*] and retroaction. The "break-in" of sexuality from the *other* implies a biological focal point, but of a very special sort. Far from the vital order resulting in sexuality through its efflorescence, it is through its insufficiency that it provokes the intrusion of the adult universe. A deficiency or prematuration of the vital order in the human infant: these are terms with which we are familiar, and which are already in Freud. They allow us to understand that, in the entirety of its extension, that "order" is infested by the sexual "order." *Infested*, but also *sustained*. Why does one so often have to force children to eat, to offer them "one spoon for daddy, one spoon for mommy,"—i.e., one spoon for daddy's love, one spoon for mommy's love—were it not that appetite is sustained, supplemented, and, to an extent, replaced in the human child by love? The proof *a contrario* lies in mental anorexia, in which a disturbance of a sexual order induces directly a disturbance of self-preservation: i.e., of the function of nourishment.

We return now to the problem of conflict. We had asked: What does sexuality attack? What, finally, defends itself against it? An initial attempt

48

at an answer by Freud: we have at our disposal a dualism of vital forces: on the one hand, "love," on the other, "hunger"; on the one hand, sexuality, on the other, self-preservation. What defends itself in this Freudian perspective is the individual struggling for his survival, a survival that would be threatened by sexuality. And it should be admitted that the existence of such a conflict, between sexual drives and the drives of "self-preservation," was constantly affirmed by Freud throughout a whole section of his writings during a certain period: such was, he tells us, "a hypothesis to which I was constrained by the analysis of pure transference neuroses." Perhaps he eventually even convinced himself of the meaningfulness of that scheme. But if the clinical writings of Freud —and of his disciples—are examined a bit more closely, it can be af- firmed that *never* was that theory in fact applied to the concrete analysis of conflict. A single brief text—"Psychogenic Visual Disturbance Accord- ing to Psychoanalytical Conceptions" (i.e., on disturbances related to hysterical blindness)—develops the idea that the visual apparatus is the site of a conflict between two functions: a function of self-preservation and a function of sexual excitation. But it must be said that, no more in this text than in any other, is the conflict *between* the two ever in fact elaborated. We are inclined to say rather that one function, self- preservation—thus, vision quite simply as function—appears in this case as the *ground* of the conflict and of the symptom and not as one of the *terms* of the opposition. More generally, it should be stated that there is a remarkable boldness and a remarkable weakness in the idea that sexuality can *in fact* threaten the life of the child and his self-preservation. What it threatens is indeed a certain integrity, but an integrity which is not *directly* the integrity of life. We should think here of the central role in Freud's theory not of death anxiety but precisely of castration anxiety as a threat to bodily unity: which is to say that what is threatened, much more than life, is *a certain representation of life*, a certain ideational representative of the vital order, which leads us at this point to the question of the *ego*.

The *conflict of the ego and of sexuality* was posed at the very beginning of psychoanalysis, in the earliest theoretical as well as clinical studies: in the *Studies on Hysteria*, the notion is constantly present. It remains to inquire what is designated by the word *ego* (*Ich*). Undeniably, there is *a certain* relation to life, a certain articulation with the preservation of the individual, or, to focus our thought more precisely, a certain relation to the *living individual* as a totality. The ego, we are constantly told—and we continue to situate ourselves in these terms in our practice—the ego is an englobing unit: we attribute to it a unitary tendency, a "synthetic func- tion"; we conceive of it as the (duly mandated or usurping?) representative of the interests of the whole.

It should be recalled—and it is a point in the history of ideas that is not without importance—that within Freud's work there is a tendency to distinguish two quite different meanings of the "ego." At times, the "historians" claim, Freud speaks of the "ego" as one speaks of it in common use, to designate simply the individual. The ego is, then, the individual as differentiated from the other, particularly the biological individual, but also the psychological individual as the site of conflict: what is at stake in the conflict, but not a participant in it. And then, one would distinguish from this rather banal and "nontechnical" sense a properly psychoanalytic meaning in which the ego, this time, is taken as a part of the totality and no longer as the totality itself, as an "agency," and, for that reason, as one of the protagonists in the conflict splitting the individual.

It is true that one can sort out on occasion—and not without arbitrariness—these two uses in Freud's writings; however, if we want to attribute to facts of language a value which is not "purely verbal," if we believe that it is never for nothing that the *same* word is used to designate two apparently different things, is not the whole problem in the relation between the two "meanings" of the same word, and must we not account for the fact that they are used in such different contexts? To move directly from this terminological question to the fundamental problem, we shall ask how an "agency," a "system," an "instance" of the personality can be charged with or delegated the functions of the individual—function being understood here in the broadest sense, to designate both elementary functions (we mentioned nourishment above) and such higher functions as "perception," "consciousness," or "thought."

We are confronted at this juncture with what we shall call, after Michel Foucault, a problem of "derivation."[1] We refer to the slippage of meaning in a concept, specifically when it moves from a certain "nontechnical" use to a new one in the realm of a science, and since it is psychoanalysis which is in question here, in the realm of psychoanalytic science. And what we should like to bring into relief is that this slippage of meaning—if it is indeed to attain a certain depth and if the thinker is original—should occur parallel to a certain slippage *in reality itself.* By this it should be understood in the specific case under consideration that the derivation is not only one leading from one meaning of the word *ego* to another (Freud having borrowed a term from common—or philosophical—thought in order to make private use of it) but that it is also (and no doubt originarily) a derivation within reality itself: the derivation within the concepts perhaps borrowed paths parallel to those of the derivation in being itself, or more exactly in the domain of *entities*, for what Freud designates by the term *agencies* are nothing more nor less than entities: the ego, but also the superego or the id.

We would posit, in this simultaneous derivation of concept and being, two dimensions, adopting in this case distinctions traditionally employed by students of the evolution of the meaning of concepts: a derivation by contiguity, habitually termed, in the technical terminology of linguistics and rhetoric, a metonymical derivation; and, on the other hand, a derivation by resemblance, or a metaphorical derivation.

What might one mean in speaking of a metonymical derivation of the "ego"? That between the ego as individual (in the "nontechnical" sense) and the ego as "agency" or element in a psychical structure, there would be a relation of contiguity or, more precisely, a relation of differentiation. The ego appears here as a specialized organ, a veritable prolongation of the individual, no doubt charged with specific functions but serving ultimately to localize something which had originally been present in the whole of the organism. What we are here designating as the "metonymical conception of the ego" represents the prevalent theoretical tendency within psychoanalysis concerning the problem of the ego. What is currently known as "ego psychology" is, in fact, a conception which makes of the ego an agency of the total person, differentiated, as is known, essentially as a function of problems of adaptation. *Ego Psychology and the Problem of Adaptation* is, in fact, the title of one of the texts inaugurating the movement; in it, the psychology of the ego is considered entirely in light of the problem of adaptation. "Ego psychology" has the merit—or at least the ambition—of wanting to reestablish the bridge between psychoanalysis and the investigations and discoveries of nonpsychoanalytic psychology, be it psychophysiology, the psychology of learning, or even child psychology or social psychology. In brief, the entire vast field of psychological knowledge and inquiry should be attached *to something* in the individual, and since we psychoanalysts have been able to dissect the individual into different parts, it should be possible to insert psychology in one of those parts; and to be sure, the part in which it can be most easily lodged is the ego. How might we define this situation of the ego as the specialized prolongation of the individual? This might be done according to three perspectives: in terms of its genesis; in terms of its situation in neurotic and psychotic conflict, thus the perspective we normally term "dynamic"; finally, in terms of the problem of the economic status of the ego, which amounts to asking what energy an agency disposes of in the midst of conflict.

Genesis: at the core of "ego psychology," there is a progressive differentiation of the "surface" of a certain apparatus upon contact with reality, a contact whose point of departure is conceived of as perception and consciousness, the privileged point of junction between the organic individual and the external world. Such a genesis entails numerous difficulties, not the least of which is knowing *what it is that is thus*

differentiated on the surface. Is it the living, biological organism? But, in
that case, what is the relation between that differentiated "surface" and
the surface of the individual, which is, in fact, constituted by his skin?
Freud attempted, not without difficulty, to establish a fairly precise
relation by recalling that in anatomy and in embryology the central
nervous system is a derivative of the cutaneous surface, or more precisely,
of the ectoderm. The observation that the skin and the central nervous
system have a common origin may have taken on for Freud a value
surpassing that of an *image*, but any attempt to press the argument to the
point of a scientific defense would rapidly lead to contradictions.[2] Or is it
rather the "psychical individual" which is differentiated, and what does
that mean? Or is it, beyond that, perhaps the psyche, what is designated as
the "id"? The hypotheses on the subject in a text that is both inspired and
strewn with difficulties—*Beyond the Pleasure Principle*—are known: we
encounter the *model* of a living vesicle whose surface, upon the impact of
shocks coming from the external world, is differentiated, forming what is
simultaneously a kind of perceptual and protective envelope. The basic
question just posed—What is differentiated on the surface?—coincides
precisely with a second one: What is a *model*? What is the meaning of the
biological model employed by Freud, the protoplasmic or protozoan
vesicle? Is it a "simple" comparison? Is it, on the contrary, something that
goes much farther, and is grounded in the very being of the subject?

Concerning *Beyond the Pleasure Principle*, we should recall that
curious series of forms embedded in each other, each with its own
protective-receptive surface:the body and the skin, the psychical apparatus and the ego, the ego itself and its crust. And since we alluded to the
difficulties of a genetic conception which presents the ego as a metonymy
of the organism—i.e., as a differentiated prolongation of it—a second, no
less difficult question would entail knowing—since among these different
levels, it is the "psychical" level that is at the center of our interest—*by
what, on the psychical level, is this impact of reality*, to which Freud
occasionally attributes so great a role, *mediated*? Need we acknowledge in
reality something like an inherent force at the level of the psyche, and
what does that mean if reality is conceived of above all as physical reality,
as the "external world"? How is that reality transformed into a "psychical" force capable of acting and of *differentiating our psyche*?

A second point of view on the ego is the dynamic one, concerning
conflict: but here again, in "ego psychology"—by which we mean that of
Freud himself as well as of his followers—the accent is once again put on
reality, in relation to conflict. Reality, in this perspective, is invested with
the dignity of a veritable agency, an agency whose effects the ego, so to
speak, would only focalize by assuring a gradual mastery of drives. We
shall quote in this context a passage from *The Ego and the Id*, a crucial

text in the turn toward ego psychology: "The ego has the task of bringing the external world to bear upon the id and its tendencies, and endeavors to substitute the reality principle for the pleasure principle which reigns supreme in the id. *In the ego perception plays the part which in the id devolves upon instinct."³*

This means that in psychical conflict an *intrinsic force* is attributed to reality. It is not so much the ego that acts through its own energies, making allowance for the demands of reality, as the real itself which seems to play the role of a veritable agency; or at least at the beginning, before the differentiation of the psychical apparatus is complete. The ego, in this view, is plugged directly into reality by virtue of the "Perception-Consciousness System" and of the first differentiated perceptual apparatuses, the sense organs. A notion like that of *Realitätsprüfung*—a notion that we believe to be far more ambiguous if followed throughout the entire extent of Freud's thought and of our experience—is taken here in its most banal sense, as a testing of reality. It thus converges with a function explored through other means of psychological investigation: learning. A testing of reality means nothing more than correcting the distortion imposed on reality by our desires. The failures of that testing of reality provide the tableau of the various psychical disturbances, be they minor (neurosis) or major and beyond doubt (psychotic hallucination). If the ego is strong enough to cause its access to reality to prevail, we are told, the hallucination is *corrected*, reabsorbed; so much so that the psychotherapy of psychotic hallucination should assume as its task the *reduction* of illusion by appealing to the limited amount of energy remaining in the ego and attempting to develop the "reality function" of the ego.

Finally, a third point in this brief panorama of "ego psychology": from the *economic* point of view, what is the energy that the ego disposes of? Here again the crucial term is continuity: a continuity with the drives of the id and notably with that group of drives that will subsequently be called, in the "final theory," life drives. These life drives are found in desexualized form in the ego; the ego is a transmitter of the id's "vital" energy, which it purifies, dominates, and channels as best it can.

In opposition to the orientation we have termed metonymical we shall situate a second conception of the ego, to be called "metaphorical." This time, the ego is not conceived of as a prolongation of the living individual but as a *displacement* of it, and of its image, to *another site*, and consequently as a kind of intrapsychical reality, an intrapsychical precipitate in the image of the individual. Is it an image of the self? It should be mentioned that several authors, probably prompted by the feeling that the purely *functional* conception of the ego leaves an empty spot in the psychical apparatus, would introduce, alongside the ego, the notion of a "self" or *selbst*. The crucial point, however, which is already indicated by Freud and renders useless and even fallacious a distinction between an "ego" and a "self," is the observation that the genesis of the ego itself is marked by the indissolubly linked image of self and other.

At this juncture, the whole field of identification opens up. And yet we will not begin with the identificatory *genesis* of the ego, to the extent that we will undertake to follow Freud's thought in its evolution. In point of fact, the notion of identification, which alone can fully account for the formation of the metaphorical agency of the ego, will be developed relatively late and incompletely. But even before Freud may have pondered, in an identificatory perspective, on how the ego came to appear, he had a kind of intuition of that *position* of the ego as an intrapsychical reality, and consequently of the both structural and economic position of the ego. In the present chapter and in the following one, we shall attempt to retrace rapidly this *metaphorical problematic of the ego* through three phases of Freud's thought. In a first stage, with that seemingly all too abstract model, the *Project for a Scientific Psychology* of 1895; then, through a far more elaborated text, the essay "On Narcissism" of 1914; finally, and more succinctly, through allusion to subsequent developments of the concept of identification.

The *Project* of 1895 is, we should emphasize once more, *the* great Freudian text on the ego, a far more focused consideration of the question than any of Freud's subsequent writings, including *The Ego and the Id*, would be. In order to situate from a structural and economic point of view the position and function of the *ego* in the text, it is first necessary to sketch rapidly the model of the psychical apparatus, or "apparatus of the soul,"[4] in which it finds its place. That model, as is known, is to all appearances neurological, since at stake is an attempt to reconstruct the totality of phenomena—the human psyche in its "normal" functioning as well as the theory of neuroses—on the basis of two fundamental hypotheses: the hypothesis of the neurone—the basis of the topographical or structural point of view—and the hypothesis of quantity—the basis of the economic point of view. Clearly these points of reference are virtually prerequisites for an entire current of rationalist and materialist thought which for centuries, if not longer, would account for phenomena on the basis of two ingredients of this kind: neurone and quantity are a new version of what in Descartes, for example, is called figure and movement, or again, in the "physicalist" school of Helmholtz that so influenced Freud, mass and energy. Freud, moreover, at the end of the nineteenth century, does not pretend that *this* is his originality: "Attempts of this kind," he emphasizes, "are common today"; and indeed it has been shown that Freud's project was not the only one to attempt to make use of the quite recent discoveries of anatomical science and the emergent physiology of the nervous system in an ambitious synthesis. Let us, however, look more closely at the text before repeating, as is common among experts on Freud, that it is Freud's first and, no doubt, last attempt to fit his entirely new psychological discovery into an old container or an inadequate mold: i.e., into a neurological theory. A Procrustean bed? A cocoon from which the resplendent butterfly will soon free itself? The model of the *Project*, we believe, is worthy of far more scrupulous attention, and we shall soon hear how modern a ring its hypotheses sound.

First, *the neurones*. They are conceived of as discrete units, entirely distinct from each other and yet entirely identical (*gleichgebaut*: built on the same model). Which allows us immediately to take a step further in the structure: since these units all resemble each other, how can they be differentiated if not by virtue of their position in the totality of the "neuronic system"? How is that position specified? By the fact that between the extremities of the neurones there are connections, and that, in addition, each neurone corresponds to a bifurcation, with an entry path and two exit paths, a scheme most simply represented by the form **Y**. The bifurcations are thus plugged into a series of successive dichotomies, constituting a network of extreme complexity.

From the point of view of their working, the essential characteristic of these neurones is their ability to convey energy. But it should be emphasized that this transmission is absolutely mechanical, entirely a function of what might be called a kind of natural slope of each neurone, which forces the energy to flow down it. In addition to this ability to convey energy, the neuronic elements are equally able, under certain conditions, to retain it, to store it up; this, because at the boundary with the following neurone is established a kind of dike, a more or less impermeable or permeable "contact barrier."

And now, *quantity*. The fact is that no specification and no description of it can be given: it is pure quantity without any element "qualifying" it. Of this pure quantity, of which nothing further will be said in Freud's writings, and which is always designated as a kind of hypothetical x, all that we know is that it is needed as an *independent* variable: along those paths combining into a complex network of conduction, something must exist that circulates and that is—at least theoretically—quantifiable, available to distinctions of more and less, of addition, removal, and discharge.

Such, no doubt, is a highly abstract and philosophical model. But we should like to emphasize that for Freud it is *also* a *clinical* model. What animates the model and makes it something different from a purely speculative construct is the clinical experience of a still emerging psychoanalysis and the rather strange phenomena it observes. This link with experience is clearly indicated from the very beginning of the *Project for a*

Scientific Psychology: "The quantitative line of approach is derived
directly from pathological clinical observations, especially from those
concerned with excessively intense ideas. (These occur in hysteria and
obsessional neurosis, where, as we shall see, the quantitative characteristic
emerges more plainly than in the normal.)"[5] We have recently encountered examples of these "excessively intense ideas"; for instance, in the
Studies on Hysteria, the face that might suddenly appear, accompanied
by what is called the affect of anxiety. And anxiety would be precisely
what comes closest to a kind of pure quantitative manifestation; it is, we
might say, an affect without quality, an affect in which nothing remains
but the quantitative aspect. The passage quoted continues: "Processes
such as stimulus, substitution, conversion and discharge, which had to be
described in connection with these disorders, directly suggested the notion
of viewing neuronic excitation as quantities in a condition of flow."
Substitution, for example, refers to the fact that an idea is capable of
taking over as its own the affect of another idea. *Conversion* concerns the
fact that a part of the body may suddenly appear to be *charged* with an
energy producing either movements or, on the contrary, paralysis;
whereas, inversely, certain ideas are found to be neutralized, almost
entirely stripped of affective resonance. *Discharge*, finally, is best illustrated by certain crises of anxiety in which the affect can, in limited cases,
become manifest in an isolated state, independent of any conscious idea.

   Ideational representative and *affect* are the elements encountered in
clinical practice, or at least the concepts permitting an optimal orientation
in the bizarre realm of neuroses. Now these two clinical notions correspond exactly, point by point, to the two basic notions in the psychical
apparatus: the neurone coincides with the ideational representative, and
quantity is the ultimate content of affect. The striking phenomenon,
revealed in the clinical exploration of neuroses, is the *independence
between idea and affect*, the possibility of a displacement of one in
relation to the other. Such a displacement between the symbol and what is
symbolized—as we saw regarding the "proton pseudos"—can, in certain
cases, be total: the symbol is capable of receiving the entire "quantum of
affect," whereas inversely, the symbolized term is so perfectly decathected
that it is finally repressed and rendered inaccessible.

   Having thus recalled the *new* and living experience that fuels the
physicalist scheme of the neuronic apparatus, we shall feel less hesitant to
allow ourselves to be drawn, after Freud, into the details of its working.
Let us juxtapose our two terms: *neurone* and *quantity*. We are in the
presence of neuronic systems, chains of successive neuronic bifurcations
that Freud also calls, without any other precaution, "mnemic" systems, by
virtue of the equivalence neurone = idea, that is the basis of his hypothesis. A mnemic system is a system of memory or memories, but with a

remarkable characteristic: *nothing qualitative is directly inscribed in it.* What is in question, of course, is a construct capable of registering "engrams," but the Freudian engram is absolutely unassimilable to an "image" or an "analagon" of the perceived object. The entire originality of a given engrammatic inscription lies solely in the specificity of the paths followed by the circulating quantity. And that specificity is limited solely to the difference between two paths or to the succession of differences, according to which, at a first bifurcation, path *a* is chosen and not path *b*, one being "facilitated" or "frayed" and the other involving, on the contrary, a "barrier"; at the following bifurcation it will be the right path and not the left that is chosen, at the third it will be the inverse, and so on.[6] It is thus *the structure of the whole,* the *sequence of these "choices" in a series of bifurcations,* that forms by itself, for each memory, a unique constellation. The resonances of such a model for a contemporary ear can be appreciated. One need barely modify or interpret it in order to see in it a kind of electronic machine, a computer functioning according to the principle of binary notation.

Neurone and quantity. The articulation of these two terms leads to the formulation of the principle governing the circulation of quantity along the neurones: such is the principle of "neuronic inertia" that we already alluded to when speaking of a kind of natural "slope" in neurones. "Neurones tend to get rid of energy": such is the first formulation of this principle. This tendency to a *complete* discharge, to *inertia,* to a *zero level* will be constantly asserted throughout Freudian theory; first, at this initial stage, under the name of the principle of neuronic inertia; soon thereafter under the term of "pleasure principle"; finally as the Nirvana principle or the principle of the death drive. At this juncture, we will not insist on the intercrossings and even misunderstandings that such an evolution will provoke within the totality of Freud's system.

At its origin, this fundamental principle is formulated with an absolute rigor: it is a matter of the neurones emptying themselves; the energy is to be evacuated completely from one element to another, as is best illustrated by the example of the symbol and the repressed term it symbolizes.[7] The affect tends to be completely evacuated, to abandon completely the ideas whose chain it travels through: such is the primary process, a kind of functioning defined as that of the unconscious, that with which psychoanalysis is concerned, as in the example of the analysis of dreams.

Once again, we shall pause here to ask in what realm of reality this principle operates. Is it the principle of a living organism? Or is it a totally different principle, situated, in spite of appearances, at a different level from that of biology? It is indeed true that Freud presents the axiom of inertia as the basic principle of every organism. And yet an organism that would initially function according to this first principle quite simply would not be viable. That is a proposition that Freud himself would perhaps not have contradicted, since he immediately invokes, in order to explain survival, a modification—an elaboration or a perfection—of the primary function into a "secondary function imposed by the requirements of life." But the contradiction comes from the fact that the incentive for this adaptative modification is sought in the primary principle itself, whereas that principle, in its essence, tends towards a leveling of every vital difference.

We would thus affirm that the principle of neuronic inertia, which in Freud's subsequent thought will become the pleasure principle, is not a principle of life and that it even has nothing to do with vital functions. And this, despite the introduction of the term "pleasure," which obviously evokes an adaptative meaning, defined in a context of psychophysiological references that we should do well at this point to sort out. *It is at the level of ideational representatives alone, and not in the functioning of a living organism that this model of a complete evacuation of psychical energy is discovered.* It is elaborated in order to account for dreams and phenomena of psychopathology. We shall return later on to the paradox implicit in Freud's postulating it, nevertheless—be it only abstractly or as a first logical phase—at the level of life. For it is a model of *death* and not of life. But it is also the model of the functioning of the unconscious.

We shall now sketch the general structure and principal characteristics of the psychical apparatus as it is described in the famous *Project for a Scientific Psychology*. That apparatus is divided into a certain number of systems, designated by the Greek letters ψ, ϕ, ω. The center of the apparatus is constituted by the ψ system, governed by the primary process and essentially corresponding to the "unconscious." This unconscious system, in which "memory traces" are registered in the form of constellations of "facilitations" or frayings, is linked on one side to external perception through the intermediacy of paths named ϕ paths. The external limit of the organism is represented on our diagram by a double line—the cutaneous barrier—but it is also the protective apparatus that, at the level of all the sense organs, filters out and reduces stimulation. On the other side the ψ system is linked to consciousness, designated as the ω system.

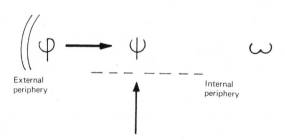

Concerning this ω system, we shall insist immediately and constantly on the fact that it has nothing to do with the ego. Finally, the ψ system (in ways far more complex than indicated in the diagram) is connected on a third side—by a whole series of devices entailing successive thresholds of reaction—with stimuli coming from within the body, whereby it receives the drive energy it is intended to discharge. [See diagram on facing page.] The ψ system, a totality of memory systems and more specifically of unconscious systems, is thus situated at the intersection of three paths: that linking it to φ and external stimuli; that bringing it certain information from consciousness; finally, through the intermediary of a kind of *internal periphery* represented in the diagram by a dotted line, the paths providing internal physiological stimuli.

If we have sketched out the diagram of this apparatus, it is by no means in order to endorse it as such and pretend to make use of it in psychoanalysis. It is solely in order to situate in it a problematic that has the strictest relations with the function of the ego: the problematic of reality and of its reproduction in the "experience of satisfaction." In this diagram, external reality is nothing else than the totality of stimuli conveyed by the perceptual apparatuses. What this diagram indicates, in its simplicity, is that the apparatus is directly plugged into external reality. At the origin of Freud's thought by no means do we find a problematic viewing the access to reality as a groping, hypothetical, and perpetually uncertain process that would start from a kind of monadic state of the apparatus. Ω, the consciousness system—although located at the very end, on the other side of ψ—emits in what might be called automatic fashion what Freud designates as the "indication of reality"; it is a kind of signal comparable to the bell in an electric marble game that rings every time a certain spot on the board is hit. When reality is perceived, there is an automatic and repetitive discharge or series of discharges informing the ψ system of the "reality value" of the stimuli it has been submitted to. It should be understood that when it is in contact with external stimulation, the central apparatus receives simultaneously two kinds of message: one (*a*) coming directly from the periphery; the other (*b*) reverberating back from ω, a message about the message that endows the first with the index "reality."

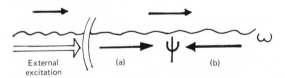

Thus do we encounter in Freud a *fundamental realism.* A naïve realism? One available for "phenomenological" interpretation? Whatever our evaluation, what is essential is to affirm that the psychical and biological individual perceives reality directly, has a sign permitting him to recognize it, and is in no need of an "ego" to accomplish any part of the process.

It is only after this model has been firmly established, and plugged into reality, that the ego will be "introduced" in a special chapter.[8] In fact, the function of the ego turns out to be necessary, not in order to accede to reality in the external world, but to discriminate between what is reality and *what would pass itself off as reality, coming from within.* In other words, the problem is that of the *internal excitation* and of its reverberation in the mnemic systems, in the systems of "ideas" already inscribed in ψ. Every internal excitation, every physiological augmentation of level of need, is translated as a revivification, in the memory systems, of traces of past experiences. Such is the process designated in the *Project,* then throughout Freud's work, by the phrase *experience of satisfaction.*

The experience of satisfaction is incomprehensible if it is not related to the biological fact of prematuration. It is, in fact, by dint of what Freud called *Hilflösigkeit*—i.e., his distress, his original impotence to help himself—that the human child cannot bring into operation the mechanisms necessary for the satisfaction of his needs, mechanisms grouped under the rubric of "specific action," which are nothing other than instinctual setups. The instinctual setups are insufficient, and in any event, they appear too late, with a gap: they are not there when one would expect: i.e., at birth. From birth onward, insofar as this gap subsists, there occurs a kind of *disqualification of the instinct*: the satisfaction of needs cannot pass through preestablished setups, that will emerge only gradually and according to the maturational rhythm of the central nervous system, but satisfaction must pass from the beginning through intersubjectivity; i.e., by way of another human, the mother. The analogy between this scheme and what we described concerning "propping" may be perceived. The signs accompanying satisfaction (the breast accompanying the offering of nursing milk) will henceforth take on the value of a fixed arrangement, and it is that arrangement, a *fantasy* as yet limited to several barely elaborated elements, that will be repeated on the occasion of a subsequent appearance of need. Freud, of course, expresses all this in terms of neuronic facilitations or frayings, since the reproduction of past experiences is not a resurgence of qualitative elements, but is limited to the fact that energy will again pass through certain paths in the system.

The problem which then occurs is the following: with the appearance of an internal excitation, the fantasmatic arrangement—of several representative elements linked together in a short scene, an extremely rudimentary scene, ultimately composed of partial (or "component") objects and not whole objects: for example, a breast, a mouth, a movement of a mouth seizing a breast—will be revivified, and that revivification, stirring consciousness (ω system) into activity is immediately relived as real. Of course, one is inclined to ask what in fact this notion of a *hallucinatory satisfaction of a wish or desire* corresponds to: is it a reality actually experienced by the infant or simply a partial model, which certainly corresponds to a structural necessity, but which, in point of fact, would be impeded by an inhibiting factor preventing it from functioning fully? It is beyond question that for Freud, this primary hallucination, or revivification of a fantasmatic trace stimultaneous with the appearance of a new need, does in fact occur during the first days of existence. "I have no doubt that the wishful activation will in the first instance produce something similar to a perception—namely, a hallucination."[9] The proof of this, of course, is the existence of dreams, the model of the primary process, in which the activation of ideas is accompanied by a feeling of utter reality.

It was precisely in order to come to terms with the problem of the hallucinatory feeling of reality that the φ-ψ-ω schema was constructed. And it is in ω, the "consciousness" system, that the impact of the process of recathecting the fantasy triggers, once again, the message or "reality sign." Beyond any simplifying mechanism, such a model implies a remarkably original conception of the "consciousness of reality": the impression of reality is not attained by approximations; reality is not learned or verified by trial and error; it is either given or not, entirely or not at all, according to whether or not the index affecting it (which is itself a discharge) is present or absent. And if the element of reality in external perception is not the result of learning, hallucinations are to the very same extent not available to being corrected by any training or experiential or testing process. *The hallucination is or is not*, and when it is, it is absolutely useless to imagine a procedure allowing one to demonstrate to the hallucinator that he is wrong. On this point, we encounter in Freud the firmness of clinical observation, rejecting once and for all a conception of the celebrated *Realitätsprüfung* as a testing of reality, as if one could go find some other reality for the hallucinator that would be capable of disabusing him.

It is at this juncture that the ego is introduced, and its role in the problem of reality will not depend on the fact that it would be plugged into reality by some sort of "direct line." From the metapsychological point of view, what defines the problem of hallucinations is the fact that there is already *too much* reality in the system, and not that a different reality must be invoked *in addition*: too much reality since there are present both perceptual reality, coming from the external barrier, and the hallucinatory reality resulting from an internal triggering of the "indication of reality," that kind of flickering signal in the "consciousness" system. To seek out an additional indication of reality which would sort out "true" reality from what erroneously passes itself off as its sign—and this, without end—would be only to renew the familiar impasses of philosophical thought. The ego, consequently, if it is the instrument of reality, does not *bring* a privileged access to the real, but by its simple presence, will permit external reality alone to function, whereas it disqualifies the pseudoreality of internal origin. Which is to say that its function is essentially inhibitive: to prevent hallucination, to cut off that "excess of reality" coming from internal excitation in order to allow the indication of reality for external perception (which had always existed without any need of an ego) to operate henceforth alone, without the rivalry of hallucinatory reactivation functioning thereafter as a valid *criterion*.

What then is the ego, charged with this function of inhibition? The ego is a part of ψ and, like ψ, is itself formed of mnemic systems; we should conclude that the ego is founded by processes that have something to do with memory: it has thus a historical origin. And yet this part of ψ seems organized differently from other mnemic systems. What predominates in the ego is not so much the fact that it is formed, like every collection of neurones, by successive bifurcations, but that it constitutes an organization, a notion evoked by the term *Gefüge*, an "organized totality," or also by the phrase *Zusammengesetztes Ich*, a "composed ego," both formed of *partes extra partes* and nevertheless unitary. Its most explicit definition has it as "a network of cathected neurones, well facilitated in relation to one another" (*Ein Netz besetzter, gegeneinander gut gebahnter Neuronen*). The notion of a *network*, in the first place, presents something more static and more closed than the image of mnemic systems whose bifurcations had as their function the evacuation of energy and not its retention. We are faced with what might be designated, anachronistically, as a kind of *Gestalt*, or form, for which the notion of an investment of energy is crucial. Whence the expression "well facilitated in relation to one another," which indicates that inside the system of the ego, communications are good, whereas on the contrary, at its periphery, there exist barriers restricting exchanges; thus the ego appears as a kind of reservoir within which functions the principle of intercommunicating pipes, allowing the energy to be distributed at an equal level, whereas, in relation to the outside, a difference of level is maintained. Doubtless, it is no accident if reference to the theory and psychology of form seems obligatory in reference to the ego, with the notions of forms charged with energy, and images and models invoking hydraulic or electric analogies: reservoir, condenser, etc. At the same time, this model of a form set off against a background evokes the relation of an organism to its surroundings, an organism which is *defined* by a limit circumscribing a region in which a certain energy circulates at a constant average level, an energy level higher than that of the external world in relation to which it is set off and against which it maintains itself.

This interpretation of the ego as a *Gestalt* harmonizes well with the mechanism described as *its inhibiting action*: there would be a kind of induction in the surrounding field, similar to that exercised by an electrically or magnetically charged mass, the induced effect being a function of the energy difference between the charge of the inducing element and that of the environment. This is what is described with precision by Freud under the term "lateral cathexis" (*Nebenbesetzung*). In order to conceive of this process in the schematic fashion proposed by Freud himself, one need only imagine, on the one hand, a neuronic path or series of paths along which the flow occurs freely, according to the primary process: i.e., a flow which is that of unconscious systems. And, on the other hand, in the vicinity of that path, a circumscribed network in which a certain energy stagnates. The inhibiting effect is produced in the first kind of path by the vicinity of the *Gestalt* of the ego, which stabilizes within its field the movement of energy and even tends to integrate it into its own system.

A lateral cathexis thus acts as an inhibition on the passage of quantity. . . . Let us imagine the ego as a network of cathected neurones, well facilitated in relation to one another. Then suppose a quantity enters neurone *a* from the outside. If it were uninfluenced it would have proceeded to neurone *b*. But it is in fact so much influenced by the lateral cathexis in neurone *a* that it only passes on a quotient to *b*, or may even not reach *b* at all. Where, then, an ego exists, it is bound to inhibit psychical processes.[10]

If it is not forgotten that what is at stake here are chains of ideas, the ego turns out to be what introduces into the circulation of fantasy a certain ballast, a process of *binding* which retains a certain energy and causes it to stagnate in the fantasmatic system, preventing it from circulating in an absolutely free and mad manner. Such is the appearance of the *secondary process*, a process which is but the result induced by the existence of an initial mass that is itself *bound*, the ego, which is literally bound by a limit, an envelope:

Wishful cathexis carried to the point of hallucination and a complete generation of unpleasure, involving a complete expenditure of defence, may be described as "psychical primary processes." On the other hand, those processes which are only made possible by a good cathexis of the ego and which represent a moderation of the primary processes may be described as "psychical secondary processes."[11]

There is thus no identity between the secondary process and the ego properly speaking. Which leads to a distinction concerning the ego between "a permanent portion" and a "changing one."[12] The fixed portion is still named "the nucleus of the ego"; within this nucleus, one cannot actually speak of the secondary process: the totality functions as a whole, the energy being distributed homogeneously at a given moment. The core of the ego is nothing but a vast reservoir acting by virtue of its charge of energy. In the vicinity of this form the mobile portion of the ego is constituted by processes on which the inhibiting influence is exercised: these are the secondary processes (the future "preconsciousness-consciousness system") and, in particular, "the thought process [which] consists of the cathexis of ψ neurones accompanied by a change in the previously operative facilitation-compulsion brought about by a lateral cathexis from the ego."[13] If we include in the ego its mobile and fluctuating field of influence, the whole of the "organization" may be regarded as capable of enlarging or contracting its boundaries: "If the level of the cathexis in the nucleus of the ego rises, the ego will be able to extend its area; if it sinks, the ego will narrow concentrically. At a given level and a given extension of the ego, there will be no obstacle to displacement taking place within the region of its cathexis."[14]

Finally, the energy with which the ego is charged is endogenous in origin: it is a part of the drive energy which comes to be stored in a constant cathexis:

This organization is called the "ego." It can easily be pictured if we consider that the constantly repeated reception of endogenous quantities in certain neurones (of the nucleus) and the consequent facilitating effects of that repeated reception will produce a group of neurones which retains a constant cathexis and which thus constitutes the vehicle for the store of quantity required by the secondary function.[15]

A constant cathexis by libidinal or drive energy; a mobility, at the periphery of a fixed nucleus, of boundaries or zones of influence, which can, depending on the case, undergo a considerable expansion or a retraction: these characteristics prefigure the descriptions of the ego that Freud will propose twenty years later.

But, in addition, the distinction within the ego of a fixed portion and a changing one allows Freud to include a valuable marginal note concerning the relation of the ego to perceptions and to objects: in the process designated as "cognitive and reproductive thought," the perceptual structure of the object is decomposed into a fixed portion—the "thing" —and a variable one—the "predicate." Now Freud notes a profound analogy between this structure of the "perceptual complex" and that of the ego: "Language later applies the term 'judgment' to this process of analysis [in the perceptual complex], and discovers the resemblance which exists between the nucleus of the ego and the constant portion of the perceptual complex on the one hand and between the changing cathexes in the pallium and the inconstant portion of the perceptual complex on the other."[16]

Now this process of analysis of the perceptual object, a truly "primary" judgment in the sense that it is prereflexive and preverbal, is valid in the first place for the perception of another human being, of a *Nebenmensch*, the prototype of all knowledge: "An object *of a similar kind* was the subject's first satisfying object (and also his first hostile object) as well as his sole assisting force. For this reason it is on his fellow-creatures that a human being first learns to cognize."[17]

Thus primary judgment would be the act through which, on the basis of "somatic experiences, sensations, and motor images of the subject's own," an initial permanence of an object is posited by means of a distinction between its "nucleus" and its "predicates." But is not the claim that this act of judgment takes place according to the primary process and without any need, so to speak, of the ego,[18] whereas its precise result is to *posit* within perception a structure analogous to that of the ego, is not that claim tantamount to sketching out the place of perceptual experiences which would found, *in the very same movement*, both the form of the ego and that of the "total object"?

4

The Ego and Narcissism

In the problematic of the ego, it has seemed to us that two paths link the ego as an individual, living totality and the ego in the sense in which psychoanalysis understands it. Of those two paths—the metonymical and metaphorical—we shall presently pursue the second one, because we regard it as the more fruitful of the two, and above all because it is the more neglected in an entire movement within contemporary psychoanalysis.

The *Project for a Scientific Psychology* of 1895 posits the ego at the outset as not being essentially a *subject*: it is neither the subject in the sense of classical philosophy, a subject of perception and consciousness (it is not ω), nor the subject of wishing and desire, that subject which addresses us psychoanalysts: it is not the whole of Ψ, nor even the essential part of Ψ, but a specific formation within the mnemic systems, an internal object cathected by the energy of the apparatus. That *object*, however, is capable of action, and it enters into conflicts as a participant by virtue of its double function: an inhibiting function or a function of binding, which we examined in the preceding chapter, and a defensive function, which we approached, in the context of the theory of hysteria, through the dual modes of pathological and normal defense. Thus no sooner have we presented the thesis that the ego is not a subject than we have to withdraw it: the ego is indeed an object, but a kind of relay object, capable of passing itself off, in a more or less deceptive and usurpatory manner, as a desiring and wishing subject.

Some twenty years after the *Project*—and about ten before *The Ego and the Id*—a crucial phase in Freud's thinking concerning the ego is marked by "On Narcissism: An Introduction" (1914). It is a text whose historical situation and meaning in what might be regarded as a structural history of Freud's thought is deserving of analysis. If one could compare the evolution of that thought to the image of a stationary, undulating motion, involving a succession of "nodes" and "loops," "narcissism" would constitute to all appearances a node, and that would be the case from a variety of points of view.

Conceived in haste, fever, and, no doubt, enthusiasm,[1] exactly like *Beyond the Pleasure Principle*, the text on narcissism, unlike that other inspired essay, quickly came to be considered incomplete, if not monstrous, by Freud,[2] and was virtually discarded before being partially misunderstood. In relation to *the totality of Freud's written work*, its situation is quite complex: it serves to confirm a whole series of clinical observations accumulated over several years on the theme of narcissism in its relations with perversion, homosexuality, and psychosis. But at the same time, in grouping these elements, it constitutes a veritable calling into question of the theory in its entirety. In addition, it should be situated in relation to the group of articles produced in 1915, and constituting the project of a kind of theoretical monument, a "metapsychology." Jones, the historian of Freud's thought, is not wrong in considering these metapsychological writings as conclusive texts, presenting a manner of synthesis and allowing of no intimation—because of any major imbalance—of the important theoretical "turning point" that would take place several years later, in 1920. Now, of these metapsychological writings, a certain number treat narcissism as something entirely surpassed, whereas others fail to assimilate it. Thus, the *concluding* texts of a whole period come *after* the calling into question and leave it, as it were, dormant, in limbo. Later, we will find not only a forgetting or partial misconstruing, but a veritable tendentious reinterpretation by Freud of his own theories when he will rewrite, in abbreviated form, the history of his "libido theory."[3]

"Narcissism" is also a focal point in that two strands which had long been separate and relatively independent—"topography" and the "theory of drives"—come to intersect in it. Hence its situation as a "nodal point," at the intersection of various lines of thought or association. Thus there evolves for the reader who, as Jones does, would like to imagine temporarily that Freud had not pursued his work any further, an impression opposed to that produced by the "metapsychological" texts of 1915: the feeling that starting from this moment of regrouping, a new development was possible, which would not necessarily pass through the detour and disruption of *Beyond the Pleasure Principle*.

Freud's thesis, if we were to condense it and, in a sense, radicalize it, would consist in three propositions: narcissism is a libidinal investment of the self, a *love of the self*—a thesis which is anything but surprising; but this libidinal cathexis of self occurs in man necessarily through a *libidinal cathexis of the ego*; and—the third thesis—this libidinal cathexis of the ego is inseparable from the very *constitution* of the human *ego*.

Freud's first move consists in "gathering what has been said elsewhere," in order to justify an introduction of "narcissism" as a psychoanalytic notion and as a generalized theory, beyond its clinical observability in certain particularly convincing phenomena. The *history* of narcissism is itself barely sketched beyond the contributions of psychoanalysis, and all reference to the ancient myth, as well as to the more recent and rather explicit work of Havelock Ellis, is completely omitted. Without wanting to take up that history, which is, at any rate, adequately retraced in volume 13 of the *Studies in the Psychology of Sex*, we shall simply note that the notion of a love of the self had long since been delineated with precision. Thus in Ovid a certain number of characteristics already emerge: the situation of narcissism as being on the nether side of sexual difference and, also, of language; Echo, that "acoustic personification of a reflection of the self" (Rank), is herself disqualified as entailing a first element of symbolization or difference.[4] In addition, "Narcissus's error" is presented in all its generality as the error of every lover, allowing for a premonition of the discovery of the narcissistic element in every love relation.[5] This is, moreover, the same direction indicated by the use certain Platonists have made of the myth of Narcissus as symbolizing the self-sufficiency of perfect love: such is the nexus that will recur when Freud himself invokes the Platonic Eros in order to designate "the life drive."

By 1898, Havelock Ellis had already mentioned several essential aspects of narcissism,[6] notably its totalitarian character, the fact that it is situated beyond autoerotic, localized sexual pleasure: narcissism would be characterized by "the tendency . . . of sexual emotions to be absorbed and at times entirely lost in self-admiration."

In opposition to the sexologists, however, when *Freud* opens his text with a reference to perversion, he has in mind no very precise nosographical entity. What counts, in this first sketch, in the rare—though exemplary —cases of "narcissism-perversion," is the resemblance which is affirmed between the subject's own body and the "body of a sexual object," treated as a whole and cajoled, contemplated and caressed; contemplation, care, and caresses are the process constituting and confirming the total form, the limit, the closed envelope of the cutaneous covering.

Outside of the "narcissistic perversion," even assuming that it can be isolated as a clinical entity (which is rather doubtful), narcissism is observed by both sexologists and analysts as a constitutive element of perversions and first of all of homosexual perversion. This allusion to homosexuality, in which Freud sees "the strongest motive regarding the hypothesis of narcissism as a necessary one," will become clearer later in our analysis upon consideration of the distinction between two types of "object-choice."[7]

A second major discovery is recalled and constantly reelaborated in the course of the essay: the crucial reference narcissism contributes to an understanding of psychosis. Two aspects, which will henceforth be orthodox, are distinguished: the withdrawal of libido and, more generally, of "interest" from the outside world—this detachment in relation to external objects, the "negative" aspect of the process, being often translated in the first stages of a psychosis by an impression and even a delirium of the end of the world—and, secondly, in correlation with this withdrawal, the necessity for this libido to be fixated to a different kind of object: internalized objects. Now Freud, unlike Jung, differentiates two degrees in this retreat of libido: a withdrawal into fantasy life—what Jung terms "introversion"—and a withdrawal into that privileged object the ego. If introversion can explain certain types or phases of neurotic existence, it is incapable in and of itself of accounting for the reversal effected by psychosis, that kind of world beyond the mirror which it creates: even if there is subsequently a recreation of a new fantasy world, it is only in starting from this radical retreat that the new elaboration will be effected. It is first of all, in an initial phase, within the sphere of the ego and within it alone that the attempt to "bind" the libidinal energy released by the end of the world occurs, and this in two apparently different forms: megalomania and hypochondria. But whether the limits of the ego be enlarged to the confines of the cosmos or, on the contrary, shrunk to the dimensions of a suffering organ; whether the libido be more or less controlled or, on the contrary, free floating, placing the subject in imminent danger of being overcome with anxiety, the psychical battle, at its beginning, is always manifest as a desperate attempt to reinvest a certain territory. A final point of reference serves as well to "underwrite" the introduction of narcissism: the evocation of the "psychology of children and of primitive peoples," a reference which claims to be clinical even as it pursues the developments of *Totem and Taboo*:

We find in children and in primitive peoples characteristics which, if they occurred singly might be put down to megalomania: an over-estimation of the power of their wishes and mental acts, the omnipotence of thoughts, a belief in the thaumaturgic force of words and a technique for dealing with the external world—"magic"—which appears to be a logical application of these grandiose premises.[8]

But here, beneath the appearance of a history of the species and of the individual, what is being introduced is the dimension of myth and of the "primal," an "originary" register which immediately, in order to be imagined, is transposed into terms borrowed from biology: "Thus we form the idea of there being an original libidinal cathexis of the ego, from which some is later given off to objects, but which fundamentally persists and is related to the object-cathexes, much as the body of an amoeba is related to the pseudopodia which it puts out."[9] And this biology would seek to be quantitative, able to account for energy balance, measures of differences of potential; so much so that at other moments a model borrowed from banking economy quite naturally seems to come into play: the protoplasmic animalcule becomes on such occasions a monetary fund, a central bank putting out or withdrawing its "investments."[10]

Primary narcissism is one of Freud's most deceptive notions, one of those which, in its apparent clarity, is most imperatively in need of *interpretation*. To simplify, we may say at the outset that there are in Freud's thought two manifest trends concerning this notion. Now the trend represented by "On Narcissism: An Introduction," if it can be detected throughout the author's work, is only intermittently dominant. It is a second line of thought, it too present from the outset, even before the introduction of the term "narcissism," and elaborated explicitly in a 1911 text, "Formulations Regarding the Two Principles of Mental Functioning," which will come increasingly to prevail. Expressed in its *manifest content*, this thesis would reconstitute the evolution of the human psyche starting from a kind of *hypothetical initial state in which the organism would form a closed unit* in relation to its surroundings. This state would not be defined by a cathexis of the ego, since it would be prior even to the differentiation of an ego, but by a kind of stagnation in place of libidinal energy in a biological unit conceived of as not having any objects. Whereby reference is made either to the prototype of intrauterine life or to the state of the nursling. Freud, in his reconstruction, persists in wanting to derive, in genetic terms, the appearance of certain "reality functions"—first of all perception, judgment, communication, etc.—from the biological monad. But he does not do so without hesitations and a remorse which is manifest even in a text as openly *psychologistic* in its orientation as the "Formulations" of 1911. It is there that we are first presented with the image of a primal state, closed in upon itself, the prototype of the state of sleep and of dreaming. The internal needs which cause a rise of the energy level in the system and would threaten its equilibrium find their outlet in "hallucinatory satisfaction." It is "the persistent absence of satisfaction" alone which would provoke—we know not how—the monad to abandon so convenient and apparently impregnable a position. Immediately thereafter, however, in a note to the same text, Freud wonders whether such an organization "could maintain itself alive for the shortest time," concedes that he is speaking of a "fiction," and refers to a model approximating this state, constituted by "the infant, if one only includes the maternal care."[11] But in this case, it seems, it is rather the imperfection of the system, the hiatus—however slight—introduced between need and maternal aid, that would provoke the hallucination. In these thoughts, Freud has, of course, no intention of presenting a concrete description of the prenatal or neonatal state, just as we have no intention of denying or affirming the effective existence of monadic biological states (the bird embryo in its egg, provided that the latter receives heat), of diadic states functioning as a quasi-monad (mother and fetus), or of far more imperfect diadic states (mother and child). The question is rather one of knowing whether we can assert the existence of a *real genesis* of the object relation by virtue of the internal pressure of need and of the path of "primal hallucination" alone. Indeed, whatever the system considered (and it should not be forgotten that it is Freud who introduces this problematic in all its abstractness), the very notion of a "primal hallucination" evokes the problem of the joining together and even of the compatibility of the two terms that define it. For, in any event, hallucination presupposes a minimal ideational content and consequently a *first* cleavage, however imperfect: a cleavage not so much between the ego and the object, or between the internal and external excitations, but between immediate satisfaction and the signs which accompany every deferred, imperfect, contingent, and mediated satisfaction: that brought by a human fellow creature.

It is the place of hallucination in relation to satisfaction which allows us best to unravel the question: do hallucinations result from dissatisfaction or, rather, cease because of it? Freud's answer is ambiguous: at times it is the drive energy accumulated by the nonsatisfaction of needs that fuels hallucinatory production; and at times, on the contrary, it is that accumulation which forces the monad to emerge from its dream. The most articulate response would no doubt be that a certain dissatisfaction finds its outlet in hallucination, but that beyond a certain energy threshold, the "hallucinatory path is abandoned." And yet, the question is precisely that of knowing what meaning to give to this notion of hallucinatory satisfaction. We can see at least two: *the hallucination of satisfaction*, i.e., the reproduction of the pure feeling of discharge even in the absence of discharge; or *satisfaction through hallucination*, i.e., by virtue of *the very existence* of the hallucinatory phenomenon. But the *hallucination of satisfaction*, assuming such a phenomenon were conceivable, could not bear within it any contradiction allowing any emergence from it, so that the objection raised by Freud himself is fully applicable here: such an organism would be destined—without any possible escape—to destruction. *Satisfaction through hallucination*, on the contrary, is quite conceivable, on the very model of dreams: the dream indeed does not *bring* the satisfaction of a wish; it *is* the fulfillment or accomplishment of the wish by virtue of its very existence. But the reference to dreams as well as the very term "wish" imply that the objective correlate of need (food) has already been metabolized into an "object," into a sign that can be introjected in its place. And in that case, the elements at play in a hallucination entail a quite different complexity and an entirely different dialectic from that which would be permitted by the so-called narcissistic monad.

All these objections, it should be emphasized, do not tend to deny the possible existence of biologically closed systems, but only underscore the contradiction inherent in any attempt to conceptualize their [subjectivity] "for itself" and, even more, to retrace the genesis of that "for itself." Primary narcissism, as a psychical reality, can only be the primal myth of a return to the maternal breast, a scenario that Freud on occasion explicitly classifies as one of the principal primal fantasies.

We have just summarized rapidly the version of primary narcissism that will become dominant, if not exclusive, from 1920 on: a version which is part and parcel of Freud's great biological myth and which, as such, should be exploited thoroughly once it has been reinterpreted. Nevertheless, in the works, over several years, that prepare the introduction of narcissism, and then, in that "introduction" itself, the meaning given to primary narcissism partially avoids the contradictions of the preceding thesis. What is posited by that term is, in fact, an originary cathexis not of the biological individual, but rather of a psychical formation, the ego; whence the conclusion, compelling in its simplicity, that if the ego is not there at the outset, narcissism, however "primary" its designation, can no more be there at the beginning than the ego. What remains to be grasped, of course, is by what necessity both narcissism and the ego pass themselves off to us, mythically, as "primal."

The notion of autoerotism in the years 1910–15 was as yet sufficiently recent in its discovery—and not yet repressed—to allow us to situate narcissism correctly in the evolution of sexuality. Autoerotism, it will be remembered, was, as early as 1905, posited not as a primal, objectless state of the human being, but as the result of a double, integrated movement: a *turning away* from functional activities which, initially, were oriented toward a certain objectality, an "object-value"; and a *turning around* of the activity on itself, in the direction of fantasy. Having established that position with apparent firmness, Freud is led, in his first statements on narcissism, to pose the following question: "What is the relation of the narcissism of which we are now speaking to auto-erotism, which we have described as an early state of the libido?"[12] And the answer is given in two short sentences, which probably contain Freud's most acute and condensed view of the question: "We are bound to suppose that a *unity* comparable to the ego cannot exist *in the individual* from the very start; *the ego has to be developed.* The auto-erotic drives, however, are there from the very first; so there must be something added to auto-erotism—*a new psychical action*—in order to bring about narcissism."[13]

Thus, what is designated as *primordial* in sexuality are the autoerotic drives, drives among which no unity exists, and we have seen how they function *in place*, based in a specific apparatus or erotogenic zone. The ego, on the contrary, is a unity *within the individual*; it is clearly posited in this text, before the "second topographical model," as an agency. Two slightly divergent terms, but perhaps complementary as well, are used to characterize the way in which it comes to be: "to be developed"—which may suggest a progressive growth—and a "new psychical action"—which evokes a specific moment in which it is established, a *mutation* through which autoerotism is precipitated into the form of narcissism. Thus narcissism is situated, chronologically or dialectically, after autoerotism, but we should recall that autoerotism, in the *Three Essays on the Theory of Sexuality*, was itself not "first": if it was indeed the first state *of sexuality*, that did not mean that it was necessarily the first *biological* state. Autoerotism was described as the phase in which human sexuality as such emerged, and was constitutive, in that sense, of the domain explored by psychoanalysis. Which is to say that narcissism, in turn, which serves to unify the functioning of autoerotism and to "give it form," would appear—however "primary"—to be prepared for by an already complex process.

Exactly like an external object, the ego is a love object, charged with libido, "cathected." What theoretical advantage is there in transposing into "economic" terms the description of feelings and passions? The point here is that the economic model—which is quantitative even if it does not provide any effective means of measurement—allows one to sharpen one's focus on certain phenomena observed in clinical practice: equivalences, exchanges, antagonisms, etc. Thus, in the theory of narcissism, it allows for a description—between the ego and external objects, or even between it and internalized fantasmatic objects—of a veritable energy "balance," in the sense that one might speak of a balance of accounts: when one is enriched, the other necessarily will be impoverished, since the individual disposes only of a *relatively constant quantity of libido*. This libidinal capital is not inexhaustible; everyone places it as best he can but cannot invest it in excess of his reserves. But in addition, despite the resemblance between a cathexis of external objects and a cathexis of the ego, there is not a complete symmetry between them: the balance is not totally reversible, for the ego will always retain a certain quantity of energy; even "in the state of being in love, when the subject seems to yield up his whole personality in favor of an object-cathexis," the ego remains the site of a permanent stasis of energy, perpetually maintaining in itself a certain minimal level.[14] This is already implicit in the comparison with the protoplasmic animalcule, which, of course, puts out pseudopodia but does so starting from a central mass which remains constant, even if maximally distended.

A second image will soon be used in the economic theory of the ego, that of a "reservoir": "The ego is to be regarded as a great reservoir of libido from which libido is sent out *to* objects and which is always ready to absorb libido flowing back *from* objects."[15] That image, moreover, will have a multiple destiny, since it will be applied first to the ego, then to the id, then again to the ego.[16] Such variations deserve better than a simple preferential choice of one or the other of them: they necessitate an interpretation, and *that* implies in turn that, as with a dream, all the elements be juxtaposed, that nothing be eliminated, and that "either/or" be retranslated as "and." What is at stake here, in Freud's hesitations is, in fact, the *actually* ambiguous status of the ego: the ego, even though it is a reservoir of the libido cathecting it, can appear to be a *source*; it is not the subject of desire or wishes, nor even the site in which the drive originates (a site represented by the id), but it *can pass itself off as such*. A love object, the ego "puts out" libido; it supplements and replaces love by positing itself as a loving subject. This thesis was already implicit in the *Project for a Scientific Psychology*, but this time it is consolidated by clinical practice, rendered concrete through a deeper analysis of the different modes of "choice" of love objects, and, finally, opened up onto the path leading to a theory of identification.

The *theory of object-choice* is undoubtedly one of the most fruitful contributions brought by the introduction of narcissism. What is at stake in it is a description of the paths, or if one prefers, of the facilitations along which the human subject comes to fix upon a particular kind of partner, or even upon a specific person. These paths may be reduced schematically to two: an *anaclitic* object-choice and a *narcissistic* object-choice. The "anaclitic object-choice" had been discovered long before and described at least as early as the *Three Essays*.[17] The discovery of narcissistic object-"choice" serves only to place in perspective and to relativize the first kind. Indeed the notion of anaclitic object-choice is essentially but a prolongation of the fundamental theory of "propping" or anaclisis as the incessantly renewed time of the emergence of sexuality. In this choice, self-preservation, the vital function, far from being in conflict with sexuality, shows it the path toward its object: "In connection with the object-choice of infants (and of growing children) what we first noticed was that they derived their sexual objects from their experiences of satisfaction."[18] With object-choice, however, a kind of repetition that is more distant from the first experiences is described: "The sexual drives are at the outset attached to the satisfaction of the ego-drives; only later do they become independent of these, and even then we have an indication of that original attachment in the fact that the persons who are concerned with a child's feeding, care, and protection become his earliest sexual objects: that is to say, in the first instance his mother or a substitute for her."[19]

Narcissistic object-choice is clearly differentiated from anaclitic object-choice in that the object is in the former case modeled on the self, that is, *on the ego*, and in that the libidinal energy is veritably *transported* rather than imperceptibly *displaced*. The two might be opposed somewhat crudely (if we chose to) as a love of the complementary, of the person who can assure life, and a love of the same or the similar; it is a similarity, however, which entails various aspects, so that the play of mirrors becomes complicated. A whole spectrum of possible narcissistic choices is presented by Freud: not only in the image of whom one is presently, but also of "what one once was—what one would like to be—someone who was once part of oneself."[20] The choice of what one "once was" is one of the more revealing, since it is the one that—discovered at the origin of homosexuality—allowed for an affirmation of narcissism not only as an "intrasubjective" position—a love of self—but as a type of object relation —love of someone who is similar to a certain image of oneself:

We have discovered, especially clearly in people whose libidinal development has suffered some disturbance, such as perverts and homosexuals, that in their later choice of love-objects they have taken as a model not their mother but their own selves. They are plainly seeking *themselves* as a love-object and are exhibiting a type of object-choice which must be termed *narcissistic*. In this observation we have the strongest of the reasons which have led us to adopt the hypothesis of narcissism.[21]

We have spoken of a play of mirrors in which a double displacement is effected: the homosexual situates himself in his mother's place, and his "object" in the place of the child he once was. If it is added that these positions are by no means stable, but, on the contrary, are caught up in a seesawlike movement which, at the slightest shift of the mirror, can cause an exchange of positions, we shall have put our finger on the fact that the models applicable to narcissism, with the complexity of exchanges they must allow, have nothing to borrow from the self-sufficient and closed form of an "egg."

Before developing certain consequences of the theory of object-choice, we shall briefly propose certain points of reference for an understanding of Freud's thought at this precise juncture. One distinction in particular is indispensable, for without it the text on "narcissism" lapses into utter confusion: it involves two terms which may appear synonymous upon superficial reading, but which are in fact borrowed from two quite different registers: *ego-drives* and *ego libido*. The ego-drives, in this text as in the entirety of Freud's work until 1920, designate the major vital functions whose aim is the self-preservation of the biological individual. As *nonsexual* instincts of self-preservation, they are constantly opposed, in a vast dualism, to the sexual drive. If we recall that libido, on the contrary, designates *sexual* drives in their energetic aspect, we see that ego-libido is situated in the other half of the dualism, designating a sexual cathexis of the ego-object in opposition to "object libido" in which sexuality cathects the "outside." In one case, consequently, we are dealing with an instinct (or drive) named as a function of its *aim* or *essence*: instinct of self-preservation or ego-instinct, on the one hand, and sexual drive on the other; whereas, in the other case, the entire distinction concerns the *object* within the same group of drives: the sexual drives or libido.

Once those two dualities have been posited, and it will be seen that they are situated at two very different levels, a problem of interpretation must once again be raised: if the distinction is to be maintained, how are we, nevertheless, to explain the ambiguity entailed by a common and almost redundant name: ego-drives, ego-libido? It is an interpretative task that brings us once again back to the general problematic we are attempting to outline here, of the passage from the ego as biological individual—as it appears precisely at the "origin" of the "ego-drives"—to the ego as an agency that can be the object of "ego-libido" and the way station of that libido in its travels: such is the entire problematic of the *derivation of the psychoanalytic ego*.

As a temporary point of reference, in order to sustain an understanding of the "introduction of narcissism," we shall propose two additional diagrams. The first attempts to represent the movement of anaclitic object-choice, and is thus the gradual opening of a gap, a progressive detachment—that might be termed *metonymical*—between different objects, as much in the contiguity of milk and breast as in the relation of part to whole: i.e., the relation of partial or "component" object (the breast) to "whole" object (the mother).

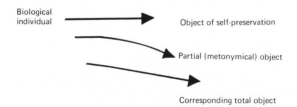

The diagram of narcissistic object-choice is quite different: here we are dealing not with a deviation or slippage, but with the rotation of a certain angle around a pivot.

The movement is reversible, and the libido can be brought at times to one and at times to the other of these objects, which are in a specular,

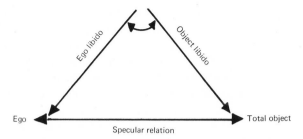

reciprocal relation. The narcissistic object-choice is thus effected through a global transference onto another site (from the "intersubjective" to the "intrasubjective" and vice versa) of energy and of the object-form which that energy maintains.

These two object-choices are presented to us only as two ideal—and, in that sense, abstract—types. Even if one is alleged to be more characteristic of the love life of men and the other of women, they in fact represent two possibilities open to every human being, even if in a particular case or at a particular moment, a specific path—narcissistic or anaclitic—is preferred, or if the two types of choice are found combined with each other in various ways. Such a meshing—in every *choice of a real object*—of metaphorical and metonymical processes should not surprise us: in more than one area, psychoanalytic investigation demonstrates that the emergence of a "psychical reality" and its consolidation occur electively at just such metaphorico-metonymical intersections.[22]

One of the remaining tasks of psychoanalytic theory is to think through the articulation of these two kinds of object-choices or of the object's "derivation." It is here that the two diagrams we proposed reveal their entirely provisional character: for by no means can one simply juxtapose or combine them. In anaclitic object-choice, in particular, the movement that is pursued beyond the partial object cannot be conceived of *solely* as a transition to "wholeness": the "whole" object is also the "counterpart" of the partial object. Thus the vectors oriented towards one's fellow human in the two kinds of choices cannot be strictly superimposed.

Freud's description of different types of love choices, whatever their diversity or complexity, leaves no doubt, however, on one point: the prevalence of narcissism, if not in every libidinal relation at least in every *love* relation, in the sense of passion: that state of loss of self that he calls *Verliebtheit*. This is clear notably in the description of object-choice in men, concerning which Freud nevertheless affirms that, in its characteristic examples, it realizes its "complete object love according to the anaclitic type." For even in that case, in fact, if the *type of object* is not modeled on the ego but chosen on the basis of the "woman who contributed her care," the libidinal energy is always borrowed from the ego, and always ready to return to it. That origin becomes manifest in *the form of the relation*, in which enthusiasm and overestimation appear as narcissistic traits. The anaclitic type in the man "displays the marked sexual overvaluation which is doubtless derived from the child's original narcissism and thus corresponds to a transference of that narcissism to the sexual object."[23] Thus the impassioned blindness of Eros—this term taken in the sense it will have in the last theory of drives, and not in that of the erotics of the *Three Essays on the Theory of Sexuality*—is the undeniable and definitive stigma of the narcissistic element existent, for Freud, in every love relation. A step further: we are even obliged to rectify the statement according to which, in the state of being in love in a man the form of the object, at least, would not be modeled on the ego. For the altruism of the lover, the "expropriation" of his own narcissism by a person in search of the love of his object, has as its precise counterpart the captivation by another "beautiful totality": the self-sufficient woman, the beautiful, narcissistic animal loving only herself. Thus at the very moment in which man—and Freud—would yield to "objectality," he shifts dialectically into another form of narcissism.[24]

This description of narcissistic object-choice in the love life of the human being ultimately allows Freud to return to the problem of *infantile narcissism*, a return that is a veritable *turnabout in perspective*. If, in an initial stage, "infantile narcissism" could be posited as an argument in favor of the hypothesis of a primary narcissism, with all the ambiguities it entailed, at this point, it is explicitly recognized that such infantile narcissism must be inferred: "The primary narcissism of children which we have assumed and which forms one of the postulates of our theories of the libido, is less easy to grasp by direct observation than to confirm by inference from elsewhere."[25] For at this juncture the perspective is reversed: it is in the attitude of the parents toward the child, "His Majesty, the Baby," that the overestimation, idealization, and megalomanic feeling of omnipotence, all characteristic of the narcissistic choice, are revealed. Freud sees in this the proof of an infantile narcissism which would formerly have been that of the parents, and to which they revert on the occasion of the birth of a child: "Parental love, which is so moving and at bottom so childish, is nothing but the parents' narcissism born again, which, transformed into object-love, unmistakably reveals its former nature."[26] The argument, however, does not win our agreement; for it sends us indefinitely from infantile narcissism to infantile narcissism, those "narcissistic states" that are alleged to be closed upon themselves, being inferred from the only observable situation: the narcissistic object-choice or *relation* of parents to child. One need go only a bit farther in the direction indicated by Freud to interpret things in the following way: reference is normally made to the narcissistic omnipotence and the megalomanic illusions of the child; but such manifestations are nothing but an inverted form of parental omnipotence. It is in terms of parental omnipotence, experienced as such by the child, and of its introjection, that the megalomania and the narcissistic state of the child may be understood.[27] Thus, in the structure of the "Introduction to Narcissism," which is at once so lacking in formalism and so rigorous, the brief description of the relation of primary narcissism is there as a call back to order, serving to correct a perpetually renewed tendency to assimilate "primary narcissism" to an objectless psychobiological state, which would have existed subjectively and effectively in an initial stage of development.

Although we have schematically opposed "On Narcissism: An Introduction" to the metapsychological writings of 1915, there is one text among the latter for which the opposition does not hold: "Mourning and Melancholia." For on the subject of melancholic withdrawal (as well as manic expansion), the discovery of narcissism as a kind of object-choice and as a mode of identification, in fact, provides an indispensable clue. Now this text confirms fully our interpretation if it is indeed true that *primary narcissism* is considered in it as *identical to the primary forms of narcissistic identification.* And that observation brings us to a second path toward situating the origin and evolution of the ego: the theory of *identification.*

At this point, we can but recall the fact that the place of identification in the whole of psychoanalytic thought has never been truly filled, despite the accumulation of innumerable clinical observations. For in spite of renewed attempts by Freud himself to define and delimit the different kinds of identification, the notion remains either too simplistic or too vague, as though it were being used to mask under a single rubric phenomena which are quite diverse. In a first—and perhaps slightly scholastic—distribution,[28] which is nevertheless apt to bring to light new arrangements, we might quite simply distinguish types of identification as a function *of what is identified with, the process in question*, and, finally, *the result.*

An identification with what? With the "object," of course, at least if that term is taken in its broadest sense. But it must further be asked whether, for example, it is a whole object or a partial object; and neither one of those terms, in turn, is simple. If identification with the whole object, what sense is to be attributed to that "wholeness"? Is it, for example, a perceptual *totum*? One is inclined to think so in the case of such identifications as those structuring the ego at its origin, but one is also forced to the conclusion that the term "whole object" designates at times—notably in Melanie Klein—something different from that arrangement: the fact, specifically, that another human can respond in a manner which is *total* or, rather, absolute, in an answer on which the child is *entirely or not at all* dependent. Similarly, when reference is made to partial identification, what is intended is not necessarily that a spatially localized part of the body (breast, phallus, etc.) is what is at stake. For there can also exist identifications with partial traits, which cannot be localized.[29] One thinks of all the identifications with character traits, for example, or even with a particular flash of personality, which is quite localized in time or space and often caught in flight, as it were, precisely because of its artificial and bizarre character. Or there may be a partial identification with an act of speech, notably an interdiction: such would be the place of so-called superego identifications, concerning which psychoanalysts insist on the founding value of utterances, "acoustical residues."

An examination of the process in play would lead us to ask if there is a common denominator among phenomena habitually classed under the same rubric: the early perceptual imprint, of which the most striking examples in animal psychology are revealed by ethology; the introjection of an object, an act modeled on a bodily process; or a type of identification referring explicitly to structure: an identification with the *position* of the other, which consequently presupposes an interpersonal interplay of relations and, as a rule, at least two other positions coinciding with the vertices of a triangle: clearly, such would be the case for oedipal identifications.

Finally, the effects or results of identifications would allow for a distinction between those that are definitive and have a structuring function, bringing about a fundamental change in the psychical being, and, on the other hand, transitory identifications: hysterical identification, the first type detected in psychoanalytic (or even pre-psychoanalytic) practice, or, in addition, what Freud later described as an identification taking place in crowds, when a group of individuals comes to place the prestigious person of a leader in the position of that agency of the personality called the ego ideal. In the context of identifications resulting in structural changes, one would also have to distinguish clearly those that are "primary" or founding, at the point of emergence of a new agency, from those that gradually contribute—through a veritable sedimentation—to shape and enrich such agencies.

In point of fact, for any given identification, object, process, and result are reciprocally and rigorously related. This is the case with the genesis of the ego, whose outline, following Freud, we have attempted to trace. The ego identification must occur extremely early if it is true that its effect is to allow for the establishment of a boundary—that is sketched out if not definitively marked—rendering intelligible such primitive mechanisms as introjection and projection: for all that Melanie

Klein has described as the dialectic of good and bad, partial and whole, the introjected and the projected, is inconceivable without the first boundary of an ego—however rudimentary it might be—defining an inside and an outside. Only that first notion of an ego provides the first oral fantasies with the minimum of terms necessary for their articulation in the "language of the oral drive": "I want to take this into me and keep that out of me."[30]

We are thus led to admit the existence of an identification that is both extremely early and probably also extremely sketchy in its initial phase, an identification with a form conceived of as a limit, or a sack: a sack of skin. The most elaborate attempt to fill in the gap left by Freud's notion of the ego, to describe that "new psychical action" capable of effecting the transition from autoerotism to narcissism, was proposed by Jacques Lacan in his theory of the "mirror stage." In it, he takes up, in particular, observations made by Henri Wallon, but gives them a far wider import. The mirror stage[31] has on occasion been misconstrued, in that an attempt has been made to render it inseparable from the experience described in it: the recognition by the infant of his shape in the concrete, technical apparatus of a mirror. Now Lacan's intention is certainly not to link in any necessary way the appearance of the human ego to the creation of the *instrument* of the mirror, nor even, for example, to the fact that like Narcissus, the infant can see his reflection on the surface of a body of water. The scenario of the child at the mirror is only the index of something that occurs, in any event, without that apparatus: the recognition of the form of another human and the concomitant precipitation within the individual of a first outline of that form.

It would be imprecise, however, to say that Freud had not himself focused on the situation of specular identification. For it is present not only in "Mourning and Melancholia" but above all in an extremely dense passage in *The Ego and the Id*, in which it is specified that "the ego is first and foremost a body-ego; it is not merely a surface entity, but it is itself the projection of a surface."[32] The observation seems enigmatic, but it is commented on in the Standard Edition in a note that received Freud's approval: "The ego is ultimately derived from bodily sensations, chiefly from those springing from the surface of the body. It may thus be regarded as a mental projection of the surface of the body, besides, as we have seen above, representing the superficies of the mental apparatus."[33] The perceptions which "partake in the emergence of the ego and in its separation from the id" are, moreover, specified elsewhere: on the one hand, as the visual perception allowing an apprehension of the body as "a separate object"; on the other hand, as tactile perceptions, the cutaneous surface having a quite particular role by virtue of the fact that the subject can explore his own body through it with another part of his body, the skin being perceived simultaneously from within and from without, and being able to be, so to speak, circumvented. The perception of pain, finally, is mentioned in this context as a last factor, and this will serve us as a pretext for recalling the constant presence, from the very beginning of Freud's thought, of a theory of *pain* that is remarkably precise and quite different from his conception of *unpleasure*. As early as in the *Project for a Scientific Psychology* in 1895, pain is accorded a special place, in particular in the context of an "experience of pain" that is considered for a while as if it were symmetrical to the "experience of satisfaction."[34] By virtue of its quality, pain is presented as "undoubtedly" different from unpleasure. From the point of view of the processes at work, it is characterized above all by the phenomenon of a breaking of barriers: "In cases where excessively large quantities [of energy] break through the screening contrivances into ϕ."[35] Thus pain is a *breaking in or effraction* and presupposes the existence of a limit, and its function in the constitution of the ego is inconceivable unless the ego, in turn, is defined as a limited entity.[36]

Freud thus indicates clearly the two meshing derivations of the ego from the "surface": on the one hand, the ego is the surface of the psychical apparatus, gradually differentiated in and from that apparatus, a specialized organ continuous with it; on the other hand, it is the projection or metaphor of the body's surface, a metaphor in which the various perceptual systems have a role to play. Of the two conceptions of the relation between the ego as psychical agency and the ego as living individual we have nevertheless given priority to one of the two: the metaphorical conception according to which the ego is constituted *outside of* its vital functions, as a libidinal object. One of the reasons for that preference stems from the psychoanalytic experience of *conflict*, for which one of the most satisfying models is that of an opposition between object-libido and narcissistic or ego-libido.[37] That opposition is close to the one found on the economic-dynamic level between the primary process and the secondary process: the primary process representing sexuality in its unbound form; the secondary process, on the contrary, relating to the "stasis" of libido in the ego and to a relative stability of love objects that itself reflects the relative stability of the form of the ego.

It remains for us, however, not to repudiate—as opposed to this conception of the ego in the image of the form of a living being—the other conception: of the ego as an organ; and to accord it its place, even if that place must, in turn, be conceived of as imaginary or delusory, partaking in *a delusion which is not simply that of the advocates of "ego psychology," but of the ego itself*. What may be observed, in fact, is a kind of reassumption of vital functions, in their feebleness and immaturity, by the ego and its libidinal support. We recalled earlier the common formula spoken by parents anxious to see their children eat: a spoon for daddy (i.e., for daddy's love), a spoon for mommy (for mommy's love). But also: a spoon for "me" (i.e., a spoon for my love, for the love of the ego), which indicates clearly the fundamental character of the narcissistic cathexis for the vital functions themselves, for the self-preservation of every human being. We recalled as well that a disturbance of love, a neurosis, can manifest itself as a disturbance of eating, as anorexia. But along with neurotic or oedipal anorexia, pivoting on "a spoon for daddy" and "a spoon for mommy," we also find psychotic anorexia, in which the problem this time is one of "a spoon for me," and consequently of a profound disturbance of the love of the ego.

But if it is true that hunger and the function of eating can be completely supported and underwritten by love and narcissism, why not consider the same situation as applicable to other vital functions, and perhaps to "perception" itself? The relation of the ego to perception, as conceived of by a certain "ego psychology," would be reversed while at the same time retaining all of its specificity. The ego does not blossom forth from the "perception system," but, on the one hand, it is formed from perceptions and primarily from the perception of a fellow creature, and, on the other hand, it takes over libidinally, as its own, the activity of perception. I perceive, just as I eat, "for the love of the ego." It will be seen that at the core of psychoanalysis there is room for a theory of the ego which, nevertheless, would have nothing in common with the classical and academic psychology that some have attempted to reinject into psychoanalytic thought. The investigations of an author such as Federn concerning the ego, its boundaries, and their cathexis, expansion, or loss indicate a possible path of relevant inquiry.

These first four chapters have attempted to show how sexuality and the ego, those two poles of the conflict with which psychoanalysis is concerned, are both connected—though in quite different ways—with what may be called "the vital order." Sexuality, in effect, leaves life out of its field of operation, borrowing from it only the prototypes of its fantasies. The ego, on the contrary, seems to take over the vital order as its own; it takes it over in its essence: constituted as it is on the model of a living being, with its level, its homeostasis, and its constancy principle. In addition, it assumes charge of the vital order by virtue of the fact that it replaces and compensates for the vital functions, so much so that ultimately, the various propositions advanced above may be summarized as "I live for my own love, for the love of the ego."

Sexuality is thus present on both sides of the conflict: "free" sexuality on one side, "bound" sexuality on the other (i.e., on the side of the ego). In the background: the phenomena of "life," but refracted and, in themselves, absent from the field that concerns us. They are there only at the horizon of the domain which is, properly speaking, psychoanalytic, perhaps even at the horizon of all that may be said about the human being.

And yet, to all appearances, it is not this metapsychology, nascent in the nodal moment of "narcissism," that Freud will develop. Or at least it will have to undergo an apparently unforeseeable mutation: that brought about by the "death drive."

5

Aggressiveness and Sadomasochism

The death drive? It is to an examination centered on that fundamentally new term, whose appearance in 1920 results in a reversal of the entire theory of drives, that our final two chapters will be devoted. Our intention is not so much to pose abstractly the question of the validity of the concept as to locate its place within the general economy of Freud's thought and, if possible, in both its diachronic and synchronic dimensions. And if at the outset we are certain that such a concept, coming at this stage of Freud's work, cannot in all likelihood be fundamentally heterogeneous to the preceding inspiration of that work nor, on the other hand, a superfluous repetition, we shall have to succeed in showing just what in the history of the work it is the return of, and by what path that return has found its derivation, and, in addition, within the simultaneity of the "doctrine" of 1920, what it is related to, and even what it counterbalances.

Since it is not our aim to exhaust so complex a task, we shall propose—in order, at least, to approach it—a provisional hypothesis allowing us to subdivide the question: at least two intentions coincide in the affirmation of the death drive, as it appears in *Beyond the Pleasure Principle*: to reaffirm the fundamental economic principle of psychoanalysis, and *that* in its most radical form: the tendency to zero; to give a metapsychological status, within the theory of drives, to the increasingly numerous and impressive discoveries of psychoanalytic inquiry concerning the register of "aggressiveness" or "destructiveness." We shall begin with this second theme.

Within Freud's thought and, more generally, within psychoanalytic practice as it developed before 1920 or even before 1915, it would be easy to make a list of those numerous places or moments in which "aggressive manifestations" may be observed: the oedipal complex, always described with both negative and positive components; love-hate ambivalence (in particular, in obsessional neurosis); negative manifestations in therapy (negative transference, resistance, etc.); sadomasochistic perversion; sadistic aspects of pregenital stages; etc. When Freud, in his role as historian of

Freudian theory, retrospectively minimizes his appreciation of such phenomena before 1920, he is able to invoke two principal arguments: the absence of any *theoretical* recognition of an aggressive *drive* and, in addition, the failure to perceive the primacy of self-aggression over heteroaggression. That retrospective view—which is partially falsified, as is invariably the case when Freud turns toward a history of his own thought—can serve as a point of departure for our considerations.

The first argument, in any event, should not be overestimated. To be sure, before 1920, not only does the aggressive drive not appear,[1] but the term "aggressiveness" itself is practically absent. But nonrecognition of an aggressive drive does not necessarily mean neglect of the theory of aggressiveness, sadomasochism, and hatred: a theory which is explicitly developed, particularly in "Instincts and Their Vicissitudes" (1915). Similarly, we are somewhat astonished to see Freud categorizing under the same heading of "affective" resistance to the recognition of aggressiveness both his own thought before 1920 and the theory of those advocates of a fundamentally "good human nature."[2] Such would seem to betray, if not an ignorance, at least an underestimation of a vast pessimistic tendency reigning both in Western philosophical and political thought and in Freud's own inspiration from their very beginnings.

And yet, the essential dimension of the affirmation of a death drive lies neither in the discovery of aggressiveness, nor in its theorization, nor even in the fact of hypostatizing it as a biological tendency or a metaphysical universal. It is in the idea that the aggressiveness is first of all directed against the subject and, as it were, stagnant within him, before being deflected toward the outside—"subject" here being understood at every level: the most elementary biological being, a protist or cell, as well as the multicellular biological organism, and, of course, the human individual both in his biological individuality and his "psychical life." Such is the thesis of "primary masochism," and there appears to be massive evidence leading us to suppose that that thesis is profoundly new, that it emerges only with the positing, in 1920, of the mythical being called the death drive. Nevertheless, without wishing to minimize the novelty of Freud's last theory of drives, we shall attempt to show precisely the tenuous but solid link binding it to the thesis evolved in 1915 from both clinical and dialectical considerations concerning the genesis of sadomasochism. That theory—which is implicit, no doubt imperfectly elaborated by Freud himself, and, above all, quickly covered over—entails, we believe, a double armature: the use of the notion of "propping" or anaclisis in the theory of sadomasochism, and the priority of the masochistic moment in the genesis of the sadomasochistic drive insofar as the latter is a sexual drive (and consequently a drive in the true sense of the Freudian *Trieb*).

If it is true that these two propositions can be rediscovered interlaced in the fabric of Freud's argument, but also that they are frequently eclipsed or hidden in it, it becomes appropriate, in order to bring them to light, to make use of a kind of index that alone gives them their relief: the distinction between the "sexual" and the "nonsexual." That distinction is explicitly posited by Freud in every text in which he studies sadomasochism: *Three Essays on the Theory of Sexuality*, already in its first edition, and in every one of its revisions; "Instincts and their Vicissitudes"; "The Economic Problem in Masochism" (1924); the *New Introductory Lectures* (1936); etc. But that opposition is not normally stabilized into an absolute terminological distinction: "sadism" and "masochism" are occasionally used, at a few lines' distance, at times to designate nonsexual violence, at others for an activity associated more or less narrowly with a sexual pleasure. A comparable "confusion" tends to reappear, even when Freud seems to want to restrict the terms of sadism and masochism to the aspect of violence that is sexualized. In such cases, he is occasionally obliged to endow the terms with a determination distinguishing them: he speaks of "sadism properly speaking" or "masochism properly speaking." At such moments, we are faced with a "terminological" problem that engages the thing itself: in our view, the slippage that Freud allows to occur within conceptual oppositions that he is perfectly aware of and that even serve as the guiding line in his argument *is nothing else than the slippage effected, within the genesis of the sexual drive, by the movement of anaclisis or propping*. But once that interaction of Freud's text and the terms it uses with the dialectic of what it describes is posited, we are obliged, as readers of Freud, in order better to control and detect the cases of slippage in operation, to force the text in the direction of a certain terminological stability: we shall consequently reserve the terms *sadistic* (*sadism*) and *masochistic* (*masochism*) for tendencies, activities, fantasies, etc., that necessarily involve, either consciously or unconsciously, an element of *sexual* excitement or enjoyment. In so doing, we shall distinguish them from the notion of aggressiveness (self- or heteroaggression), which will be considered as essentially nonsexual. This preliminary distinction in no way prejudges the actual existence of a nonsexual aggressiveness, and inversely, it does not invalidate a priori the proposition that behavior commonly called "sadistic" may, in fact, spring from nonsexual instinctual components.[3]

If, as we believe, the Freudian theory of "propping" should be used as the guiding scheme in understanding the problem of sadomasochism, it is important to recall briefly two major aspects of that theory: the marginal genesis of sexuality and the genesis of sexuality in a moment of turning round upon the self. On the one hand, indeed, propping implies that sexuality—the drive—emerges from nonsexual, instinctual activities: organ pleasure from functional pleasure. Every activity, modification of the organism, or perturbation is capable of becoming the source of a marginal effect, which is precisely the sexual excitation at the point at which that perturbation is produced. Propping is thus that leaning of nascent sexuality on nonsexual activities, but the *actual* emergence of sexuality is not yet there. Sexuality appears as a drive that can be isolated and observed only at the moment at which the nonsexual activity, the vital function, becomes detached from its natural object or loses it. For sexuality, it is the reflexive (*selbst* or *auto-*) moment that is constitutive: the moment of a turning back towards self, an "autoerotism" in which the object has been replaced by a fantasy, by an object *reflected* within the subject.

If the theory of propping came to be relegated increasingly to a secondary role and even repressed, this is understandably even more the case for its application to the problem of masochism. And yet two of Freud's major texts, "Instincts and Their Vicissitudes" and "The Economic Problem in Masochism," clearly bear its imprint. Those two texts are separated by the turning point of 1920, but despite that separation, a quite remarkable convergence, perhaps unperceived by Freud himself, may be discovered between them. "Instincts and Their Vicissitudes" examines, as is known, fundamental modifications that can be studied as forming their own dialectic, within the drive itself, regardless of the fact that these "vicissitudes" may give rise to defense mechanisms. Concerning sadism and masochism, there are two contiguous "vicissitudes" that come into play: "reversal into the opposite" and "turning round upon the subject." The reversal into the opposite, for example, would be the change in a drive from active to passive, or vice versa, which leads to the conception of a kind of complementarity between the two positions, just as one can move grammatically from an active to a passive proposition through a simple, reversible "transformation." The "turning round upon the subject," on the other hand, concerns the "object" of the drive, an object that can be exchanged and—though formerly external—become an internal object: the ego itself. Freud notes at the outset, however, that in the transition, sadism to masochism, the two vicissitudes are intimately interconnected and can be distinguished only abstractly.

Freud's text, in its great density, progresses like a spiral, presenting a whole series of approximations and schemes that do not invalidate each other but gradually come to complete the image of a common "genetic" structure. In addition, the scheme presented for the "pair of opposites" voyeurism-exhibitionism would also have to be considered, as Freud suggests. Before entering into some detail concerning Freud's *schemata*, we shall indicate what is at stake in the question. Historians of Freud's thought, and Freud himself, admit that after 1920, what is considered as the initial stage is the reflexive, masochistic moment: to make oneself suffer or to destroy oneself. It is from this "primary masochism" that —through "turning round"—both perverse sadism and masochism would be derived: to find someone else capable of making one suffer. Before

1920, on the contrary, and particularly in "Instincts and Their Vicissitudes," it would be the activity directed towards an external object—sadism—that would be first (destroy the other, make him suffer, aggress him), whereas masochism would only be the turning round of this initial attitude, a turning round that is, moreover, easily understandable in terms of obstacles encountered in the external world and, above all, of the guilt caused by aggression.

Now this turning round upon the self is not unknown to us within the vicissitudes of *sexuality in general*, since it is just such a process that constitutes the transition to autoerotism. But we know that within that autoerotic turning round, there is a kind of hiatus, deception, or slippage, whose result is that the *activity which turns round upon the subject is not the same one that was directed toward the external world* but a "derivative" of it (according to a complex movement of metaphorico-metonymical derivation). Thus, sexual activity breaks loose while turning round from a nonsexual activity directed towards a vital object. If, then, we would show that Freud's theory of sadomasochism conforms to the scheme of propping, it will be by bringing into focus:

(*a*) that the first active phase, directed towards an external object, is designated by Freud as sadistic in a manner that can only be regarded as improper, or by extension—since what is in question is a stage that is nonsexual—and is thus, properly speaking, aggressive or destructive;
(*b*) that sexuality emerges only with the turning round upon the self, thus with masochism, so that, within *the field of sexuality*, masochism is already considered as primary.

We shall present successively three schemes of derivation, or, as Freud would put it, three *vicissitudes*: a double turning round, active form–reflexive form–active form; a turning round with reversal into its opposite, active form–reflexive form–passive form; finally, a double symmetrical derivation, which, starting with the reflexive form, can result in the active as well as the passive form.

1. The central passage of the entire text is one which shows destructive activity turning round into masochism, and the latter again becoming the point of departure for sadistic activity.[4] But the text can be used only if we interpolate into it our own commentary and, through that commentary, the distinction, at every juncture, between what is nonsexual activity and what is linked to sexual pleasure. By means of that distinction (which merely follows Freud's quite clear indications), the passage finds its only possible interpretation in terms of the theory of "propping":

Our view of sadism is further prejudiced by the circumstance that this drive, side by side with its general aim (or perhaps, rather, within it), seems to strive towards the accomplishment of a quite special aim—

[Thus at the outset the problem of the dual nature and the dual aim of sadistic activity is posited.]

not only to humiliate and master . . .

[the aims of aggressiveness]

but, in addition, to inflict pains . . .

[a properly sexual aim, and consequently sadistic "properly speaking"]

Psychoanalysis would appear to show that the infliction of pain plays no part among the original purposive actions of the drive . . .

[Thus what is primary is an aggressiveness that is directed outward but not sexual. That instinct is the one that Freud calls the "instinct to master," or the tendency to make oneself the master of one's fellow being in order to achieve one's ends, but without that action—which could be characterized as entirely instrumental—implying any sexual pleasure in itself.]

A sadistic child takes no account of whether or not he inflicts pains, nor does he intend to do so . . .

[Here, we are obliged to substitute, for the "sadistic child," the "aggressive child." For the child is alleged to destroy what he finds in his path, without that destruction in itself being what is intended, nor for that matter the subjectivity of the other (i.e., his pain), and even less the pleasure discovered in the other's pain. It is of little concern to us, moreover, whether this description of the child, as a simple force of nature, seeking to accomplish its aims and breaking everything in its way, is the description of an actual—however fleeting—stage, or the positing of an ideal moment: in any event, what is presented is an ideal genesis.]

But when once the transformation into masochism has taken place . . .

[Thus the turning round of the aggressiveness onto the self; but here "masochism" is taken in its literal sense, at once sexual and nonsexual.]

the pains are very well fitted to provide a passive masochistic aim; for we have every reason to believe that sensations of pain, like other unpleasurable sensations . . .

[It will be seen that Freud distinguishes clearly, within the general domain of unpleasure, the quite specific phenomenon of pain, and that it is *pain that is linked to the essence of masochism.*]

trench upon sexual excitation and produce a pleasurable condition, for the sake of which the subject will even willingly experience the unpleasure of pain . . .

[Thus pain is a perturbation like any other perturbation; like all those which Freud had already begun listing in the *Three Essays*, it can be an "indirect source of sexuality," in the same way as, for example, physical exercise or intellectual effort. The idea of "trenching" upon the domain of sexual excitation effectively evokes the "marginal" character of this production of pleasure.]

When once feeling pains has become a masochistic aim, the sadistic aim of *causing* pains can arise also, retrogressively . . .

[This time, we should read: "sadistic, properly speaking," in the sexual sense, since what is being considered is the emergence of a new aim that did not exist in the initial active phase of pure destructiveness.]

for while these pains are being inflicted on other people, they are enjoyed masochistically by the subject through his identification of himself with the suffering object . . .

[Thus, whether what is under discussion is fantasy or sexuality, in both cases the masochistic moment is first. The masochistic fantasy is fundamental, whereas the sadistic fantasy implies an identification with the suffering object; it is within the suffering position that the enjoyment lies.]

In both cases, of course, it is not the pain itself which is enjoyed, but the accompanying sexual excitation—so that this can be done especially conveniently from the sadistic position.

[Here Freud is attempting to elude the difficulty of "enjoying pain" by displacing the problem; but the formula "enjoying the excitation" leads to the same impasse, at least if it is considered from the "economic" point of view. We shall return to this question later.]

The enjoyment of pain . . .

["In both cases," thus one's own pain as well as the other's pain.]

would thus be an aim which was originally masochistic . . .

[And there we have the whole of "primary" masochism.]

but which can only become the aim of a drive . . .

[To become a drive in the proper sense of the term is to become sexuality.]

in someone who was originally sadistic.

[Unless we are prepared to eliminate every possible interpretation of this passage, we shall have to resolve to redefine "sadistic" once again as "aggressive": the sadomasochistic sexual drive, the enjoyment of pain, has its origin in the masochistic phase, but on the basis of a turning round of a primary heteroaggressiveness.]

In the same spirit as Freud's in the text under discussion, we shall schematize below this first vicissitude with its double turning-round:

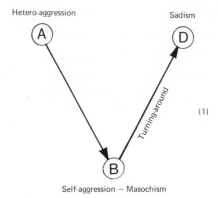

2. A second scheme is presented which, through various slight altera-tions, is interesting in its specification of the transition from sadism to masochism. The latter, on this occasion, is presented to us in two different aspects: "what is commonly termed masochism," which implies passivity toward an extraneous subject; and an intermediate stage in which "there is a turning round upon the subject's self *without* an attitude of passivity towards another person."[5] The three stages are thus:

(*a*) "The exercise of violence or power upon some other person as its object," an activity that Freud terms sadism, but in which, it is specified, sexuality does not enter into play.

(*b*) A turning round upon the self: "The active voice is changed, not into the passive, but into the reflexive, middle voice."[6] This is self-inflicted torment, which is not yet true masochism.

(*c*) Passive masochism, in which the active aim is transformed into a passive aim, which implies the search for another person as "object" (object of the drive, but subject of the action).

The first appearance of the sexual component, through propping, is linked to the turning round of the aggressiveness into self-aggression, so that it is always the reflexive "self-" phase to which the emergence of sexuality corresponds. We should note as well that during this reflexive phase the object is lost and is regained only in the fantasmatic doubling (in phase *b*) and then in the search in phase *c* in which the inversion of active and passive roles intervenes.[7]

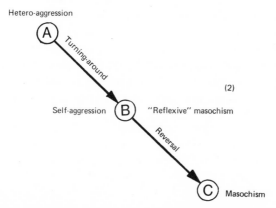

3. Finally, a third and rather different model is presented concerning the vicissitudes of the "scopophilic drive." At stake is the genesis from the middle or reflexive position of the two active and passive positions. What one finds is not a reversal, but a kind of primary position, constituted by the "autoerotic" phase. The active position would result from the search in the external world for an extraneous object capable of being substituted for the original object, whereas the passive position would have an extraneous person substituted for the subject himself.

We reproduce this scheme below, first in its application to the scopophilic drive:

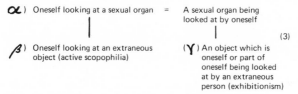

and then transposed into more abstract terms:

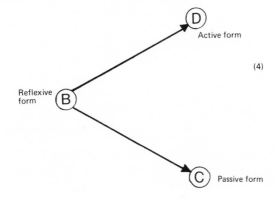

What should be observed is that Freud envisages the possibility of applying such a scheme to the case of sadomasochism, i.e., to derive from it the active and passive forms of a primally reflexive position. No doubt he explicitly dismisses this possibility, although conceding that "it might not be altogether unreasonable."[8] This scheme indeed *seems* to him to be in contradiction with the previously affirmed priority of heteroaggression. In the choice between a priority of the active relation to the object and a priority of the reflexive or "self-" phase, we rediscover a familiar debate that we have already evoked: is what is first a reflexive, objectless state closed in upon itself, as our last diagram seems to indicate, or, on the contrary, a would-be primary relation to the object? Now, our entire interpretation has tended to show that this is a false debate, and that the two statements are quite reconcilable, to the extent that they are not located on the same level: Diagrams 3 and 4, which derive everything from a primal reflexive phase, are located entirely on the level of sexuality: in the problem of the scopophilic drive, already in reflexive phase α, what is in question is "looking at a *sexual organ*" or "a *sexual organ's* being looked at." On the contrary, in the sequences moving from the active form to the reflexive form and from there either again to activity (Diagram 1) or to passivity (Diagram 2), we progressed from an initial stage which was, strictly speaking, nonsexual, since sexuality emerged only in the second stage. All of this might be expressed by saying that the transition from A to B is located in the *genesis* of sexuality, whereas the subsequent transformations, starting from B, represent the *vicissitudes* of sexuality.

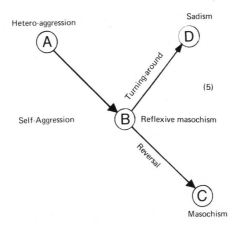

We have consequently taken the liberty of combining and even superimposing the various diagrams suggested by Freud's successive analyses, first by situating them on the same level, as in Diagram 5, then in a three-dimensional model intended to bring into relief the existence of two different surfaces—self-preservation and sexuality—and to bring into play the process of propping as the line at which the two surfaces intersect (see Diagram 6).

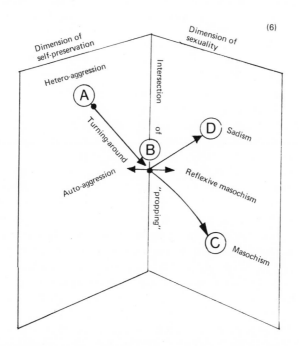

Such a diagram reveals clearly just how the problem of primary masochism is posed by Freud, and how the hesitations he proliferates —and eagerly bears witness to, for instance in the notes appended after 1920 to the text of "Instincts and Their Vicissitudes"—lag considerably behind what had already (and from the outset) been evolved in his thinking on sexuality, an idea that did not and will not vary, whatever form is taken by the notion of (nonsexual) aggressiveness.

The counter-proof of our interpretation might be found in a text of Freud's that takes up the same question: "The Economic Problem in Masochism."

We are in 1924. The great metabiological opposition of death drives and life drives constitutes from this point on the basis for any Freudian consideration concerning a problem of origins. At the beginning, the unsurpassable presence of two great opposing forces, at work from the start within, must be postulated. It is therefore all the more striking to note that this metaphysical postulation does not prevent Freud from beginning his consideration of *erotogenic masochism* by recalling the first thesis concerning the emergence of sexual excitation:

In my *Three Essays on the Theory of Sexuality*, in the section on the sources of infantile sexuality, I put forward the proposition that sexual excitation arises as an accessory effect of a large series of internal processes as soon as the intensity of these processes has exceeded certain quantitative limits; indeed that perhaps nothing very important takes place within the organism without contributing a component to the excitation of the sexual drive. According to this, an excitation of physical pain and feelings of distress would surely also have this effect.[9]

It is this "libidinal sympathetic excitation" that would provide the physiological foundation of erotogenic masochism.

The reader will recognize in the notion of *sympathetic excitation* (*Miterregung*) the exact counterpart of the "marginal action" or "marginal gain" by which Freud very early defined "organ pleasure" in relation to the functional pleasure in which it takes support. No doubt this explanation is considered "insufficient," and Freud will immediately refer to the great ontological struggle between destruction and libido. And yet, if it is true that "we never have to deal with pure life-drives and death-drives at all, but only with combinations of them in different degrees,"[10] it is indeed one of those alloys, "primary erotogenic masochism," that is first for us, and this erotogenic masochism emerges through the phenomenon of "sympathetic excitation": "Another part [of the death or destructive drive] is not included in this displacement outwards; it remains within the organism and is *'bound' there libidinally with the help of the accompanying* [*sympathetic*] *sexual excitation mentioned above*: this we must recognize as the original erotogenic masochism."[11]

No doubt the fruitful notion of propping will gradually be replaced by the more abstract and mechanical notion of fusion and defusion (*Mischung/Entmischung*) or by the all too convenient commonplace of "erotization." The crucial point, however, is that its place remains staked out at the same spot in the development of the drive: in the stage in which self-aggression is transformed, in place, into reflexive masochism.

We shall soon have to inquire into the thesis that such self-aggression, for its part, is an original datum and not the result of a turning round. But at present we are following a different line of thought that is closer to Freud's first intuitions concerning sexuality. Those intuitions posited autoerotism as a second stage, following a turning round or a brushing back of a self-preservative activity that was initially directed outwards. Now, if the genesis of reflexive masochism is to be understood as a turning round upon the self, that turning round must still be examined, for it is proposed to us in two different senses: first of all, self-aggression can be conceived of as an actual or even physiological process: domination or conquest of oneself. Freud proposes that general direction by evoking, in "Instincts and Their Vicissitudes," the virtual existence of a reflexive phase from which would emerge both sadism and passive masochism: "It might not be altogether unreasonable to construct such a [preliminary] stage out of the child's efforts to gain control over his own limbs."[12]

The other possible meaning of this turning round would be, to all appearances, quite different, since it would entail an internalization of the whole of the action on the psychical level, a process of an entirely different order from a real activity (e.g., of the muscles), since what would be implied would be a fantasmatization. And yet in the general description of autoerotism, these two types of internalization were already encountered: the withdrawal to an erogenous zone and brushing back into fantasy. These two modalities would seem not to be reducible to each other: one could be described in terms of sheer behavior or physiology; the other implies the dimension of "interiority." *Introjecting the suffering object, fantasizing the suffering object, making the object suffer inside oneself, making oneself suffer*: these are four rather different formulations, but our practice shows the subject constantly moving from one to the other. An author like Melanie Klein takes seriously (as well one should) the apparent absurdity of those equivalences and of that movement, entailing a mode of thought that would adhere with maximal fidelity to the experience of psychoanalysis—without introducing into it a logic of the excluded middle—and would posit the identity of the internalized object and the fantasy of the object.[13] But in that case, we are obliged to admit that a fantasy, the introjection of the object, is a perturbation and, in its essence (wheher its "content" be pleasant or unpleasant), a generator of autoerotic excitation.[14] Similarly, as an effraction, the fantasy is the first psychical pain[15] and is thus intimately related, in its origin, to the emergence of the masochistic sexual drive.

In order to illustrate this process of a "turning back into fantasy," we should like to evoke the analysis undertaken by Freud, in "A Child Is Being Beaten" (1919), of the genesis of a sadomasochistic fantasy. It turns out to be a veritable clinical confirmation of "Instincts and Their Vicissitudes," since in it we follow the development of a drive through the dialectic binding the successive versions of the ideational representatives or fantasy to which the drive is attached. We encounter the vicissitudes of the drive, or perhaps even its genesis, if the distinction proposed earlier is accepted.

We shall recall the three phases of the evolution of the beating fantasy, as Freud describes them in women and more specifically in neurotic (mostly obsessional) women:

1. My father is beating the child whom I hate.
2. I am being beaten by my father.
3. A child is being beaten.

The third phase corresponds to a symptom that is confessed, not without difficulty, in the course of the analysis. For convenience of exposition it can itself be analyzed into the following two aspects: on the one hand, its accompaniment in "affect" and "discharge," and, on the other, its ideational content. The two manifestations regularly accompanying the evocation of the fantasy are an intense sexual excitation, almost always leading to masturbatory gratification, and a violent feeling of guilt, apparently related to the masturbation but, more profoundly, to the ideas evoked. As for the "fantasmatic representation" itself, it entails an imagined scene according to a relatively unchanging scenario, none of which prevents each of the three terms (beater/beaten/the action) from being relatively undetermined or variable, borrowed as each is from an undefined series of possible paradigms. As in the case of every fantasy, it should be emphasized, we are dealing with an imagined scene, particularly in its visual aspect. The sentence "A child is being beaten" is the way in which that scene is transposed by the subject in the discourse of therapy, and by Freud himself in his presentation. And yet that transcription into the language of words has the merit of bringing to light the grammar of the fantasy itself, and, in what follows, Freud's analysis will be based (just as in "Instincts and Their Vicissitudes") essentially on the successive modifications of the utterance of the fantasy.

"A child is being beaten": the intentional indeterminacy of the proposition manifests the neutrality that the patient would maintain in relation to the elements of the scene: "The figure of the child who is producing the beating-fantasy no longer itself appears in it. In reply to pressing inquiries patients only declare: 'I am probably looking on.'"[16] It may be noted, moreover, that the French translation, "On bat un enfant," inverts the position of the subject and object in relation to the German formula: "Ein Kind wird geschlagen." We note this, not in order to point out an imprecision in translation, but, on the contrary, to indicate that at this stage of the fantasy, there is an indeterminacy or in any event a reversibility between the active and passive formulations:

One beating child = child being beaten by one.

Inevitably, one thinks here of the equation proposed by Freud in order to translate what he called the reflexive stage of the scopophilic fantasy.[17]

The series of three formulations recalled here is presented by Freud as a chronological sequence. The first two phases, unlike the third, have to be rediscovered in the course of the work of analysis. But at this point a fundamental difference appears between phases 1 and 2: phase 1 may be remembered in the course of the analysis; phase 2, on the contrary, has to be reconstructed: "This second phase is the most important and the most momentous of all. But we may say of it in a certain sense that it has never had a real existence. It is never remembered, it has never succeeded in becoming conscious. It is a construction of analysis, but it is no less a necessity on that account."[18]

It is precisely on the difference in nature between phases 1 and 2 and on the transition between the two that we shall insist in order to reveal clearly in them the process of a turning back into autoerotism:

Phase 1 corresponds to one or several real scenes, in the course of which the child may have actually seen her father mistreat a little brother or sister: "One may hesitate to say whether the characteristics of a 'fantasy' can yet be ascribed to this first step towards the later beating-fantasy. It is perhaps rather a qestion of recollections of events which have been witnessed, or of desires which have arisen on various occasions."[19] As opposed to this, phase 2 is entirely fantasmatic; it is the first phase of the fantasy properly speaking, a point which Freud underlines by designating as the "original fantasy" (*ursprüngliche Phantasie*) the scenario "I am being beaten by my father."[20]

Phase 1 is consciously remembered, rediscovered through an investigative effort pursued in common by Freud and his patient. We may, in fact, doubt that it was ever truly repressed. As opposed to this, phase 2 is profoundly interred in the unconscious and generally inaccessible.

Finally, the first phase is barely sexual, or rather, to take up a term already used in the context of the "seduction theory," it is "sexual-presexual." If we accept a terminological distinction advanced above, its bearing is aggressive and not, properly speaking, sadistic:

Doubt remains, therefore, whether the fantasy ought to be described as purely "sexual," nor can one venture to call it "sadistic." . . . So perhaps we may say in terms recalling the prophecy made by the Three Witches to Banquo: "Not clearly sexual, not in itself sadistic, but yet the stuff from which both will later come." In any case, however, there is no ground for suspecting that in this first phase the fantasy is already at the service of an excitation which involves the genitals and finds its outlet in a masturbatory act.[21]

As opposed to this, the unconscious fantasy "I am being beaten by my father" is masochistic in the proper sense of the word: it expresses in "regressive" form the fantasy of sexual pleasure obtained from the father. The presence of sexual excitation already in phase 2 is attested to for Freud by the fact that certain patients "say that with them masturbation made its appearance before the third phase," which "inclines one to assume that the masturbation was at first under the dominance of unconscious fantasies and that conscious ones were substituted for them later."[22]

It may be seen that it is in the transition to phase 2 that *the fantasy, the unconscious,* and *sexuality* in the form of *masochistic excitation* together emerge in a single movement. In addition, in the fantasmatic *content*, the transition from phase 1 to phase 2, entailing a "turning round upon the subject," encourages us to recall the diagram of the *genesis* of the sado-masochistic drive:

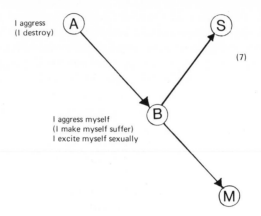

and then to inscribe in it the Freudian statements:

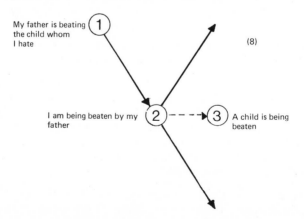

To be sure, the application of the general model to the case of the beating-fantasy cannot be purely mechanical. There remain discordances and discrepancies; but these, far from being totally irreducible, turn out to be fruitful for further considerations.

1. In phase A, characterized as heteroaggressive, it was *ego* (the individual in question) that was the subject of the action. In "A Child Is Being Beaten," in 1, it is "my father" who is doing the beating.

This difference does not seem essential to us. Ego wants to destroy the person in his way, the obstacle to his "self-preservation," and it matters little, at this precise level, whether he does it directly or through another person. Between father and ego, there is a kind of implicit transitivism, which should be distinguished scrupulously, moreover, from a fantasmatic introjection. The important point is that the essential aspect of the action is situated on the level of vital or "egoistic" interests: "The fantasy [in its first phase] obviously gratifies the child's jealousy and is dependent upon the erotic side of his life, but is also powerfully reinforced by the child's egoistic interests."[23]

2. But we proceed only further into paradox by insisting on the aggressive, nonsexual aspect of the first phase; what is considered as presexual, linked to self-preservation and the "egoistic" tendencies is what Freud openly designates as the parental complex or the oedipus complex! In a purely chronological interpretation, we would arrive at the following absurdity: far from its being the case that the oedipal comes from sexuality, it would be sexuality which comes from the oedipal, which would itself allegedly take place on an initially presexual level, that of self-preservation or of "tenderness." The notion of a regression to the anal-sadistic stage, invoked in this text by Freud in order to account for sexualization, would only reinforce the absurdity if we limited ourselves to a purely linear chronology: the nonsexual oedipus complex would take on its sexual meaning through regression to an earlier stage of the libido.

An extended discussion of this question would necessitate a highly complex ordering of the different modes of temporality with which we deal in psychoanalysis, and would go beyond the limits of our inquiry. What is important for us, in the present paradox, is to emphasize that the so-called sequence of *propping* functions according to a temporality that it is impossible to superimpose on any other (that of sexual stages or that of the structuring of the object or Oedipus); newly formed sexuality seems able to take as its point of departure *absolute anything*: the vital functions, to be sure, but also, ultimately, the "oedipal" relation itself in its entirety, taken as a natural relation with a function of preservation and survival.

Moreover, what confirms this interpretation is that the oedipal complex is approached by Freud obliquely in this context, from a particular angle: from the point of view of drives, what is in the foreground is not the erotic relation, but the relation of "tenderness"; but above all, in the structure, the triangle under consideration is not the oedipal one: ego (little girl)-father-mother, but the triangle of rivalry, called in other circumstances the "fraternal complex": ego-parents-brother or sister.[24]

3. This clinical example afforded Freud the opportunity to examine the problem of repression from various points of view: the relation of repression to regression, the relation of repression to sexual role, masculine or feminine, and so on. We shall simply add a remark intended to render explicit the identity of the *object* on which repression bears: it is essentially on the second phase, or on the fantasy at its emergence. It is, nevertheless, quite common to speak of repressed childhood memories, and not without clinical basis. In fact though, *what is repressed is not the memory but the fantasy derived from it or subtending it*: in this case, not the actual scene in which the father would have beaten another child, but the fantasy of being beaten by father. And yet it is clear that the repression of the fantasy can drag along with it into the unconscious the memory itself, a memory which after the event [*après-coup*] takes on a sexual meaning: "My father is beating another child—he loves me (sexually)." Just as the object to be refound is not the lost object, but its metonym, so the "scene" is not that of the memory, but that of the sexual fantasy derived from it.

4. Finally, we have situated, in the position of what we called reflexive masochism, or the middle voice, a fantasy which, however, has a properly masochistic content in the "passive" sense: I am being beaten by my father. But that is because, as we have emphasized, the process of turning round is not to be thought of only at the level of the content of the fantasy, but *in the very movement of fantasmatization*. To shift to the reflexive is not only or even necessarily to give a reflexive content to the "sentence" of the fantasy; it is also and above all to reflect the action, internalize it, make it enter into oneself as fantasy. To fantasize aggression is to turn it round upon oneself, to aggress oneself: such is the moment of autoerotism, in which the indissoluble bond between fantasy as such, sexuality, and the unconscious is confirmed.

If we press that idea to its necessary conclusion, we are led to emphasize the privileged character of masochism in human sexuality. The analysis, in its very content, of an essential fantasy—the "primal scene" —would illustrate it as well: the child, impotent in his crib, is Ulysses tied to the mast or Tantalus, on whom is imposed the spectacle of parental intercourse. Corresponding to the perturbation of pain is the "sympathetic excitation" which can only be translated regressively through the emission of feces: the passive position of the child in relation to the adult is not simply a passivity in relation to adult activity, but passivity in relation to the adult fantasy intruding within him.[25]

6

Why the Death Drive?

Although there is little likelihood that the contents of the article "The Economic Problem in Masochism" will disappoint its reader, the title does raise expectations that are only partially fulfilled. The essential part of the text is devoted to a series of developments and quite fascinating reformulations: the description and analysis of the different clinical forms in which masochism may become manifest in analytic experience. But only the first pages of the text are devoted to the difficulties and contradictions inherent in the very notion of masochism. Moreover, the "solution" proposed barely invokes any clarification of the notion, and is based on the distinction between the life drive and the death drive, to which two different principles of operation would correspond: the pleasure principle and the Nirvana principle. Thus the "economic problem"—indeed the essential paradox—in masochism was quickly emptied of its content and relegated to the level of a primordial opposition between "love" and "strife," that titanic struggle of which we know from experience only the muted and inevitably ambiguous derivatives, since we can only encounter "combined" forms.

It is not even certain that the introduction of the "death drive," rather than illuminating the difficulties of masochism, does not, on the contrary, compound them, with the result that, among the numerous paradoxes generated by masochism, two in particular appear as fundamental: one seems inherent in the very notion; the other is generated by the articulation of masochism with the death drive.

THE PARADOX OF MASOCHISM

If we accept the definition "the pleasure of unpleasure," the *paradox inherent in masochism* lies in the very contradiction of those terms. From that point of departure, solutions—are they the evasions of reason or the evasions of the subject itself?—are conceivable only through the introduction of a difference of register between the terms of the equation, or through some conceptual slippage from one to the other of the terms.

One might attempt to resolve matters by situating each of the two terms in a different *place* in the topography of the subject, according to the well-known formula "What is pleasure for one system is unpleasure for another one." One could press the formulation further by assuming that one of the agencies (the superego) derives its pleasure *from the very fact* of inflicting unpleasure on another agency (the ego). That theory is normally quite compatible with common sense, for which the pleasure of sadism would be in no need of any special explanation, but would be fully "understandable." If, in the sadistic scenario, the pleasure is in the subject and the unpleasure in the object, the introjection of the latter and its integration into an agency of the personality (the ego) would result in an *internalization of the entire scene*, thus accounting at minimal expense for the paradox of masochism; the masochist would achieve enjoyment only through his fantasmatic identification with the active pole of the scene. That "solution," which would seem to be a matter of course as soon as it is admitted that every individual is divided within himself and against himself, was never proposed by Freud, however, who always considered *the pleasure of causing suffering* as more *enigmatic* and requiring a more complex explanation than *the pleasure of suffering*: which is to say that the "superego pleasure" just invoked can by no means serve as an irreducible and unquestionable axiom. But above all, it should be recalled that the coexistence within the same individual of pleasure and unpleasure, related to each other but assignable to two different "sites," is one of the most general of psychoanalytic discoveries. Clearly, in the case of any subject in analysis—be he "psychosomatic," "neurotic," or whatever—we encounter a certain suffering, and the movement of therapy consists in showing how that suffering is provoked by the individual himself, in the name of a search for pleasure in another site. To characterize such a conjunction, in every individual, as masochism or moral masochism is tantamount to diluting the very notion of masochism and perhaps even of depriving it of any meaning at all. Not that a masochistic potential, prepared to be reawakened and to reinforce suffering of any origin, does not exist in every human being. But it remains that the subject is masochistic only insofar as he derives enjoyment *precisely there where* he suffers, and not insofar as he suffers in one place in order to derive enjoyment in another, as a function of some arithmetic or algebra of pleasure. This may also be formulated as follows: the subject suffers *in order to* derive enjoyment and not only *in order to be able* to derive enjoyment (or to pay the "tax" for enjoyment).

At this point we are thus led to seek out, within the persistently disquieting equation pleasure = unpleasure, a slight hiatus that would be introduced simultaneously within the domains of pleasure and of unpleasure. If for reasons of convenience, we designate the two members of the equation as a positive pole and a negative pole, we can continue to state that positive = negative only if the "positive" is not quite a positive, and the "negative" not quite a negative. Or rather: the "negative" is not quite the negative of the positive it is opposed to.

On the negative side, first, the notion of suffering or, more interesting still, the phenomenon of *pain*—as an effraction of the boundary and a rush of "unbound" energy—may be substituted for the notion of unpleasure.

On the positive side as well, distinctions are proposed which are not facilitated by established terminology and in particular by the German term *Lust*, traditionally translated as "pleasure" or occasionally as "enjoyment," but including as well the meaning of "lustful desire." We should introduce, in addition, the notion of *satisfaction*, which refers to the appeasement linked to a reduction of tension and is thus situated entirely within the "vital" register. But in that case, within the positive pole, pleasure would seem to divide into two directions: on the one hand, enjoyment [*jouissance*], in the sense both of frenetic pleasure and of lust, and on the other, satisfaction, understood in terms of the allaying of vital tensions. Within that opposition, the term "pleasure" may be used—depending on the author, and, in the case of Freud himself, at different times—to refer to one pole or the other of the fundamental opposition: either it is situated in opposition to functional satisfaction (and in that case, what is being referred to is the pleasure of the drive: for example, what Freud calls "organ pleasure"), or it is opposed to frenetic "enjoyment" [*jouissance*] (and in that case pleasure would be situated on the side of constancy and homeostasis):

Satisfaction/pleasure ~ pleasure/frenetic enjoyment[1]

We shall now make use of the results arrived at precisely through an interpretation and repositioning of Freud's theses:

1. Two levels must be scrupulously distinguished: the quantitative series or scale: (functional) pleasure—(functional) unpleasure; and the level of lust and/or enjoyment.

2. It is at this second level, lust and/or enjoyment, that the thesis of primary masochism is situated. It might be formulated as "the lust for and/or the enjoyment of pain." It is intimately connected with the notion of fantasy as an alien internal entity and with the drive as an internal attack, so that the paradox of masochism, far from deserving to be circumscribed as a specific "perversion," should be generalized, linked as it is to the *essentially traumatic nature of human sexuality*.

3. There remains the question raised by the formula lust and/or enjoyment, in which the terms are posited in a complex relation of both conjunction and disjunction. Certain of Freud's formulae, in their

appearance of imprecision, may indicate a fruitful path at this juncture: "The subject derives enjoyment from the excitation," wrote Freud in "The Economic Problem in Masochism," perhaps thus posing the entire problem of the sexual drive; and, in the *Three Essays* of 1905, concerning the very "sources" of the sexual drive: "The concepts of 'sexual excitation' and 'satisfaction' can to a great extent be used without distinction, a circumstance which we must later endeavor to explain."[2] "Deriving enjoyment from excitation": that expression situates Freud in a line of thought that long predates him, one affirming that "man prefers the hunt to the actual capture." Ought we simply to say that the hunt *also* entails within it the fantasy of the capture? But that formulation would be banal and inadequate if we failed to realize that the fantasy is no longer the same, is not the simple reflection or image of the capture, and is *derived* from it through a complex series of displacements. Such would be, in the most general terms, the relation between lust and "satisfaction."

"Deriving enjoyment from excitation"; "lust and/or enjoyment": these formulae lead us to inquire as to what value—at the level of that "mechanics" or "hydraulics" of ideational representatives which characterizes human sexuality—may be attributed to economic concepts derived metaphorico-metonymically from the register of biological homeostasis. The paradox compounded by the introduction of the notion of the death drive into the problem of masochism will guide us in what follows.

THE ECONOMIC PARADOX
OF THE DEATH DRIVE

Beyond the Pleasure Principle, which in 1920, one year after "A Child Is Being Beaten," introduces the death drive, remains the most fascinating and baffling text of the entire Freudian *corpus*. Never had Freud shown himself to be as profoundly *free* and as audacious as in that vast metapsychological, metaphysical, and metabiological fresco. Terms which are entirely new appear: Eros, the death drive, the repetition compulsion. Old and apparently forgotten ideas, in particular those of the *Project for a Scientific Psychology*, are taken up again and renewed. More than ever, the problem of Freud's "biologism" exercises, in this text, a global pressure: what is the function of the recourse to the life sciences, manifest at times as unrestrained speculation, at others, as a series of references to precise experimentation? A dialectical move "beyond" *Beyond the Pleasure Principle*, if it is to be convincing, will be possible only after the meaning of that biologism has been elucidated. Finally, concerning the questions more directly approached in our two previous chapters, we find in this text a new, entirely original, and even unheard-of conjunction of the different modes of what might be designated, in all its generality, as the "negative": aggression, destruction, sadomasochism, hatred, etc.

Profoundly baffling, Freud's discourse is only sporadically and super-ficially subordinated to logical imperatives: it constitutes a mode of thought that is free (in the sense of free associations), is undertaken "in order to see," and implies a series of "about-faces," acts of virtual repentance, and denials. *That* (equally attractive) counterpart of the freedom of Freud's style of inquiry may well disappoint the reader who fails to identify with that style: the holes in the reasoning constitute so many traps; the sliding of concepts results in blurring terminological points of reference; the most far-reaching discussions are suddenly resolved in the most arbitrary manner. If one resists the inherent movement of the text, one may derive the impression that every question in it is poorly posed and in need of reformulation.

Seductive and traumatic as it was, the forced introduction of the death drive could only provoke on the part of Freud's heirs every conceivable variety of defense: a deliberate refusal on the part of some; a purely scholastic acceptance of the notion and of the dualism: Eros-Thanatos on the part of others; a qualified acceptance, cutting the notion off from its philosophical bases, by an author like Melanie Klein; and, most fre-quently of all, a passing allusion to or a total forgetting of the notion.

Beyond the Pleasure Principle, in two distinct *frescoes* or *canti*, draws us irresistibly towards its myth: in a first phase, the most varied manifes-tations of *repetition*, considered as their irreducible quality, are attributed to the *essence of drives*. In a second movement, the tendency of the human individual to reproduce his earliest states and objects is related to a universal force largely transcending the fields of psychology and even life itself: a cosmic force that would irresistibly bring more organized forms regressively back to less organized ones, differences of level to a generalized equality, and the vital to the inanimate.[3] At stake then is an effort to grasp what is most "driven" in the drive—ataraxy, Nirvana as the abolition of every drive—and what is most vital in the biological—death, explicitly designated as the "final aim" of life. Every living being aspires to death by virtue of its most fundamental *internal* tendency, and the diversity of life, as observed in its multifarious forms, never does anything but reproduce a series of transformations determined in the course of evolution, a series of adventitious detours provoked by any one of a number of traumas or supplementary obstacles: the organism wants not simply to die, but "to die in its own way."

As opposed to the "universal" of death, concerning which we are, however, hard put to imagine what could conceivably restrict it, a second principle, is, nevertheless, necessarily posited: the *life drive* or *Eros*, a tendency, which, despite certain of Freud's denials, contains within it a measure of the optimism borne by the ideology of progress or evolution: Eros is the gatherer and tends to form perpetually richer and more complex unities, initially on the biological level, then on the psychological and social one. Finally, as opposed to the principle of energy-entropy, that has been plausibly compared to the death drive, Eros tends to maintain and to raise the energy level of the configurations whose intimate bond it forms.

Exactly like Thanatos, however, Eros is an *internal* force, inherent within the individual: atom, cell, living individual or psyche. It is within that monad that the dialectic or, rather, the fierce struggle between the two primordial forces unfolds; secondarily, a part of the primal destructiveness is deflected towards the external world, giving rise to the manifestation we identify in phenomena as aggressiveness. Thus, to return to the question already debated in "Instincts and Their Vicissitudes," what is affirmed here is the primacy of self-aggression over heteroaggression, that self-aggression being, in turn, only the consequence of the absolute primacy within the individual of the tendency towards zero, considered as the most radical form of the pleasure principle.

But what is posited in this case as primary within the individual combines, under a common rubric, tendencies which are hardly compatible: the reduction of tensions to zero (Nirvana), the tendency towards death, self-aggressiveness, the search for suffering or unpleasure. From an economic point of view the major contradiction consists in attributing to a single "drive" the tendency towards the radical elimination of all tension, the supreme form of the pleasure principle, and the masochistic search for unpleasure, which, in all logic, can only be interpreted as an increase of tension.

With an analytic sharpness, an originality of clinical observation, and a dialectical sense which are all characteristic of his work, Daniel Lagache has inquired into the "situation of aggressiveness" in a brief text.[4] It is an important point of reference for an understanding of the author's own thought, but also for sorting out the different meanings that mesh in the notion of aggressiveness. The concept of the death drive is considered in the essay as "the formal unity of several ideas that are related but not identical." Within this virtual monster (in the sense in which beings created by human fantasy, chimeras or dragons constructed out of the most heterogeneous bodily parts and members, are so designated), Lagache enumerates various ideas, with the intention of criticizing them one by one, proposing a plausible interpretation of them, and finally resituating them in a different region of theory or experience. He thus examines:

1. The tendency towards a transition from the organic to the inorganic, in which he detects the most speculative and specious aspect of Freud's argument. He finds for it a possible application at a purely descriptive level within clinical practice: in order to designate a kind of reification of the subject—elsewhere termed psychical inertia or viscosity—in which routine and sclerosis have replaced, in a lasting or even definitive manner, renewal and creativity.

2. The tendency toward a "reduction of tensions." It is a notion that Lagache accepts, provided it not be pressed to the absurd, that is, to its extreme form as a reduction of *all tension*. When thus restricted, it constitutes within the author's personal problematic one of the poles of human activity, in opposition to the tendency toward a "realization of possibilities": two principles of psychical life which alternate, fuse in more or less harmonious compromises, or oppose each other according to type of conflict or stage of life. Between these two principles, psychoanalysis need not choose.

3. Finally, primary masochism, a notion concerning which Lagache first looks for psychophysiological illustrations or equivalences, but which he ultimately interprets as the initial state of the infant, totally dependent on another for his satisfaction. "Primary masochism" would thus find its place within the "narcissistic masochistic position," one in which the notion of masochism is assimilated a priori by the author to those of passivity and dependency.

To criticize, in the etymological sense of the term, is to choose, to redistribute the cards, to "air out" what has been mixed. In that sense, Lagache's criticism is one of the most far-reaching and relevant of those applied to the domain of aggressiveness. And yet, such a conception of criticism and analysis is, in our opinion, incomplete, if one intends to approach *as a psychoanalyst* a concept posited by the very founder of analysis. It goes without saying that with the death drive, there was a poor deal of the cards; the hand is all wrong. But is it sufficient, in that case, to begin the deal all over again and to effect a more correct combination? We believe that it is insufficient simply to redistribute the cards without first attempting to interpret the previous "deal." To analyze, to interpret: we have attempted to sketch the outlines of what might be an undertaking of this type, a project which is not that of any "pathography"—the interpretation of the individual desire of someone (Freud, in this case) through reference to the biographical traces he left—but an interpretation of what, in a work, allows for an intuition of the unconscious, even though it is already at the level of discursive thought: a theoretical exigency, the refracted derivative of desire.[5] Exigency? We would willingly adopt instead a Freudian term, that of *Zwang*: the compulsion, constraint, or demoniacal force of which one of the most striking examples is the *Zwang* of the oracular message irrevocably determining the destiny of Oedipus.[6]

Of those great compulsions of thought that periodically resurge within Freud's creation, the death drive is the most glaring and perhaps the one that combines all the others. How can one fail to note, with Jones, the manifest characteristics of this *Zwang*? In 1920, a text appears that was written out of the same inspiration marking the discontinuous and syncopated series of other writings that were similarly produced in a kind of second state: from the *Project for a Scientific Psychology* to "On Narcissism: An Introduction." But here a completely new development originates, situated outside any predictable trajectory: outside of the continuity of the metapsychological writings of 1915 and of their system, which seemed on the brink of attaining closure; divergent as well from the calling into question entailed by "narcissism," since what is at stake is not so much consolidating that entity as shattering it. A hypothesis emerges that calls everything into question. A hypothesis? It is presented without restraint, with arguments of every kind, frequently borrowed from fields outside of psychoanalytic practice, calling to the rescue biology, philosophy, and mythology. The argument progresses through a series of interruptions, obstinately following the details of a scientific debate only in order to abandon it abruptly, like an unlucky gambler who suddenly kicks over the table. We are thinking here of the extremely long and highly documented discussion of the problem of the immortality of the living cell in the light of experiments on protista, in which abruptly, when the reader has the impression that an examination of the various theses would end up refuting the existence of an *internal* tendency towards death, Freud breaks off his argument with an *ad hoc* invocation of the metaphysics of entities:

It becomes a matter of complete indifference to us whether natural death can be shown to occur in protozoa or not. . . . The drive forces which seek to conduct life into death may also be operating in protozoa from the first, and yet their effects may be so completely concealed by the life-preserving forces that it may be very hard to find any direct evidence of their presence. . . . But even if protista turned out to be immortal in Weismann's sense, his assertion that death is a late acquisition would apply only to its *manifest* phenomena and would not make impossible the assumption of processes *tending* towards it.[7]

This hypothesis is presented under cover of an extremely "liberal" argument: the universal right to pursue a train of thought as far as one wants, the sovereign freedom to philosophize and to dream.

Soon, however, the *Zwang* appears; the metaphysical reverie becomes dogma, as much for Freud as in relation to his disciples: "To begin with it was only tentatively that I put forward the views I have developed here, but in the course of time they have gained such a hold upon me that I can no longer think in any other way."[8]

A second and opposite index of the same *Zwang*: this veritable dogma, which seems ineluctable at the level of the systematicity of Freud's thought, has only a relatively slight repercussion on the totality of his work as soon as that work moves closer to clinical practice: the new "dualism" is poorly integrated into the theory of conflict, in which the old oppositions of drives subsist, while the death drive is invoked as a last recourse and generally remains in the background: "Theoretical speculation [as opposed to "empirical analysis"] leads to the suspicion that there are two fundamental drives which lie concealed behind the manifest ego-drives and object-drives."[9]

Similarly, when, in *The Problem of Anxiety*, Freud reexamines the theory of neuroses, he integrates the death drive into the oedipal conflict only in the form of hatred, without according it any place insofar as it is self-destructive. Even though the theses of Rank on the "birth trauma," which are extensively discussed in that text, might have served as a pretext for the idea of a primordial internalization of destructiveness, the hypothesis of a primary death anxiety is ultimately discarded and the absence of death on the unconscious level reaffirmed.[10]

In speaking of the "hold" upon him exercised by the notion of the death drive, and thus authorizing us to propose the term *Zwang*, Freud himself opens up the path to attempts at interpretation. Jones, for his part, as Freud's biographer, sketches out such an analysis, but in a direction that one cannot but regard as reductive. It should be recalled in his favor that in so doing he was following certain indications given by Freud himself concerning the interpretation of philosophical works:

Psychoanalysis can indicate the subjective and individual motives behind philosophical theories which have ostensibly sprung from impartial logical work, and can draw a critic's attention to the weak spots in the system. It is not the business of psychoanalysis, however, to undertake such criticism itself, for, as may be imagined, the fact that a theory is psychologically determined does not in the least invalidate its scientific truth.[11]

Thus Jones juxtaposes bit by bit objections concerning the intellectual "content" of the work, and the psychoanalytic interpretation as a function of the biographical elements at his disposal. The dichotomy itself already is dubious, but one's impression of inadequacy is compounded upon examination of each of the two terms: no doubt Freud's personal position in relation to death—his own as well as that of those close to him—is deserving of attention even in its slightest details—but analytic neutrality, which should be the rule for such a leveling of "material," is hardly to be found in the opinion that thinking "of [death] every day of [one's] life . . . is certainly unusual."[12]

Such naïveté or prejudice—which, in our opinion, by no means disqualifies every attempt at analytic psychobiography—finds its complement in an insufficiency of theoretical awareness. In this area, Jones *isolates*, in fact, two "turning points" in the same period: the revision of the conception of the psychical apparatus, resulting in the "second topographical model," in which the author would see only a crowning or felicitous perfecting of Freud's work; and the introduction of the death drive, in discontinuity with the whole of Freud's earlier elaborations, in which the irruption of an emotional attitude that had been repressed too long would have only the import of a symptom. Ultimately, a certain cast of rationalistic mind, which may be analytic, but is profoundly antidialectical, results only in isolating and fragmenting: in separating—with the possibility of subsequently juxtaposing—the basic criticism from the psychological interpretation; in splitting the theory into good and bad innovations without imagining that there might exist a structural tie between them; and finally, in neglecting to relate the compulsion of the death drive to everything that prefigures or prepares it in other configurations within Freud's work.

Although our project is to interpret, at the level of Freud's work, the *Zwang*, the exigency governing this paradoxical turning point, it will be impossible for us to support that interpretation by following in detail the relevant texts, in particular *Beyond the Pleasure Principle*. We are thus compelled to present, with a minimum of justification, the elements in it that *recur*, and whose energy serves to propel the concept of the death drive. In our opinion, there are three of these.

The first element is what we have called the priority of the "self-" or *selbst*- phase: the reflexive phase. That primacy, within the field of psychoanalysis, is manifest as much in the theory of autoerotism as in the presupposition of primary narcissism, conceived of as that state which is totally closed in upon itself and which offends both theoretical considerations and the most elementary data of observation.[13] We shall simply add, in this context, that within *Beyond the Pleasure Principle*, the life drive or Eros, the force that maintains narcissistic unity and uniqueness, can be deduced as a *return to a prior state* only through an appeal to mythology: the fable of the androgyne, proposed by Aristophanes in Plato's *Symposium*. So will it go as well for the death drive: here, the priority of the reflexive phase, which was solidly affirmed concerning *masochism in the sexual sense*, will begin proliferating or fissioning in relation to origins: already at the level of the self-preservation of living beings, aggression was there "in place," stagnating *within*, and it is "in place," "'bound' there libidinally with the help of the accompanying sexual excitation" in the form of primary masochism.[14]

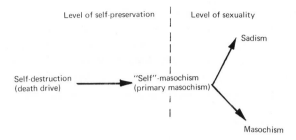

The second element of the exigency of the death drive is the *priority of zero over constancy*. As is known, Freud's statements on the pleasure principle refer it—as if to its objective or even mathematical foundation—to the constancy principle. But *the duality of pleasure*, which splits it into functional pleasure and into organ pleasure, into calm satisfaction and into frenetic enjoyment [*jouissance*], is rediscovered at the economic level. The formulations of the constancy principle give the impression of masking, in turn, the same duplicity. We may cite, in illustration, two definitions of that economic principle in *Beyond the Pleasure Principle*:

(*a*) the tendency to "the reduction, constancy, or removal of internal excitation";
(*b*) the tendency of the psychical apparatus "to maintain as low as possible the quantity of excitation present within it, or at least to maintain it at a constant level."

Thus the terms "zero" and "constancy," which we would separate, are often presented by Freud as situated on a continuum, either by establishing between them a vague synonymy, with "psychophysiology" receiving the task of distinguishing between them more clearly, or else by presenting the tendency towards constancy as a "makeshift" replacement for an absolute reduction of tensions.

And yet at this quantitative level, in which Freud introduces a terminology that is, to all appearances, mathematical, an a priori discussion of the different relations possible between the two terms is justified:

1. *Can zero be assimilated to constancy?* Imagine a simple homeostatic system, in which a self-regulating mechanism has as its function the maintenance of a certain energy level N. In such a system, depending on whether it strays from level N by excess or by lack, what will be needed to reestablish the homeostasis is either an evacuation *or* an influx of energy. Moreover, an energy reduction tending to bring the system to level zero will, for part of its way, appear as favorable for the reestablishment of constancy, but pushed to its extreme, it seriously contradicts the constancy principle.

In relating this to the level of the homeostasis of an *organism*, we encounter the experimental evidence that a living being does not seek—as Freud would have it—only to evacuate excitations which would be perpetually brought to it from the outside: that organism, depending on circumstances and on its internal energy level, can just as well be in quest of "excitation" as desirous of avoiding it or evacuating it.

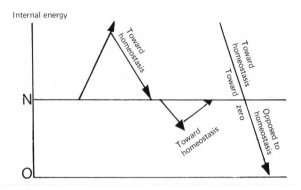

Thus, insofar as they are related within a single system to the same type of quantifiable energy, a zero principle and a constancy principle are irreducible to each other.

2. *Can a zero principle be considered as second in relation to a constancy principle?*

Consider once more the same homeostatic system, but introduce this time a second variable: along with the internal energy, the *quantity of deviation* in relation to reference level N, whether that *deviation* be

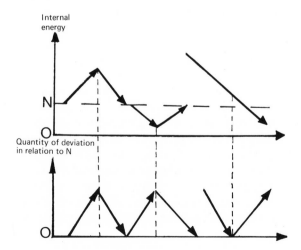

produced by the diminution of the absolute amount of energy or by its increase. In that event, a single energy exchange between the system and its environment will manifest itself differently depending on which of the two variables is being considered: the law of constancy, posited as governing the variations in time of absolute quantities of internal energy, will be translated into a zero law when it is the *quantity of variation or divergence* in relation to the norm which is itself taken as a variable (see diagram on p. 114).

These considerations bring us directly to the thought of Fechner, three of whose theses should be considered as basic points of reference in discussing Freud's considerations on the economy of pleasure: *the statement of the pleasure principle;*[15] *the statement of the stability principle*, considered by Freud as the equivalent of his constancy principle;[16] finally, the fundamental *psychophysical law* that quantifies "sensation" as the "logarithm of excitation," thus establishing a precise relation between the quantity of variation that can be subjectively perceived (a quantity defined by the sums of successive divergences) and the quantity of the objective rush of energy. Now Freud's position in relation to these three crucial contributions of Fechner is quite remarkable: He does not say a word about Fechner's statement of a "pleasure principle of action" in terms rather close to his own conceptions. He considers the "stability principle" as the most general statement of "the tendency which we attribute to the mental apparatus . . . and that is subsumed as a special case under Fechner's principle."[17] He declares that "G. T. Fechner held a view on the subject of pleasure and unpleasure which coincides in all essentials with the one that has been forced upon us by psychoanalytic work," and quotes an extremely explicit passage in which Fechner applies to the sensations of pleasure and unpleasure the fundamental "psychophysical relation."[18] And yet he refuses, on that basis, to follow the path that would allow him to relate, in a precise function, the tendency towards zero to the tendency towards constancy, the zero of perceived divergence to the constancy of the internal energy level.

In order to unravel his own definition of the constancy principle, Freud, working in the same direction as Fechner, would have had to distinguish two entirely heterogeneous kinds of quanta: the quantum of divergence in relation to stability (which Fechner terms sensation) and the quantum of energy (which Fechner terms excitation). Now from the outset, in his earliest pronouncements on "economics," Freud's thesis refers to *only one kind of "quantity"*: in the *Project for a Scientific Psychology*, the internal quantities (Qn) are of the same kind as the external quantities (Q) and are differentiated from them only by virtue of the diminution imposed by a system of filters; elsewhere, and constantly, terms like "quantum of affect," "sum of excitation," "external stimulation," "internal stimulation," etc., are given as purely and simply homogeneous.

3. Thus Freud rejects Fechner's solution. He needs a quantum of *materially* detachable psychical energy, capable of circulating, and not that *mathematical function*—Fechner's "sensation"—which is inseparable from the "excitation" whose logarithm it is. But above all, what he needs to affirm, against all biological or psychophysical plausibility, is the *primacy of zero in relation to constancy.*

As early as the *Project for a Scientific Psychology*, the distinction between the two principles that will later appear in the form of the Nirvana principle and the constancy principle is clearly posited: we have already come across the first of those principles under the name of the "principle of neuronic inertia": "Neurones tend to divest themselves of quantity." And it is once again explicitly asserted as a tendency towards zero excitation: "Its original trend toward inertia (that is, towards a reduction of its level of tension to zero)."

This *zero principle* is constantly identified with the following notions:

(*a*) free energy, tending towards discharge by the shortest paths;
(*b*) the primary process;
(*c*) the pleasure (or unpleasure) principle: "Since we have certain knowledge of a trend in psychical life towards *avoiding unpleasure*, we are tempted to identify that trend with the primary trend towards inertia. In that case *unpleasure* would coincide with a rise in the level of quantity or with a quantitative increase of pressure. . . . *Pleasure* would be the sensation of discharge."[19]

It will be seen that in this definition of pleasure-unpleasure, *within the psychical apparatus, the question of constancy is irrelevant.* Not that a principle of constancy is absent from Freud's earliest elaboration; but it is to be found in an entirely different position, *in opposition to* the primary process. The notion of constancy is introduced secondarily, as an adaptation, on account of "the necessity of life," of the principle of inertia:

The neuronic system is consequently obliged to abandon its original trend towards inertia (that is, towards a reduction of its level of tension to zero). It must learn to tolerate a store of quantity sufficient to meet the demands for specific action. In so far as it does so, however, the same trend still persists in the modified form of a tendency to keep the quantity down, at least, so far as possible and avoid any increase in it (that is, to keep its level of tension constant).

Thus the *law of constancy*, even if it is not explicitly posited as a principle, corresponds quite precisely to bound energy and the secondary process. We had already identified it earlier as linked to the emergence of *the agency of the ego*, a form cathected at a constant level and serving to ballast, moderate, and regulate the free circulation of unconscious desire, inhibiting the hallucinatory recathexis of ideational representatives linked to the first "experiences of satisfaction."

And it is quite true that with *Beyond the Pleasure Principle*, it is the same priority of zero which, under the name of Nirvana, is being reaffirmed. The displacement of the term "pleasure principle" should not mislead us: the pleasure principle, insofar as, throughout the text, it is posited as being of a piece with "its modification" as the reality principle, is henceforth situated on the side of constancy. It is "its most radical form" or its *"beyond"* which, as the Nirvana principle, reasserts the priority of the tendency towards absolute zero or the "death drive."

But Freud's thesis would be only a rehash if it did not bear witness to another aspect of the *Zwang*: *the necessity of inscribing the two preceding priorities (the priority of the self-phase, the priority of zero) within the domain of the vital.* Starting with *Beyond the Pleasure Principle*, it is the whole of the biological domain, its history as well as its contemporary manifestations, which are infested by the immanence of a tendency to zero, working obscurely but ineluctably "within."

Shall we invoke a romantic or Rilkean theme bearing witness to Freud's permanent familiarity with his own death? Perhaps. But the carrying over of zero into life and the attempt to *deduce* the living from it are manifestations that are not without precedent within Freud's theoretical work itself.

To the extent that the *Project for a Scientific Psychology* is presented, in the most total metaphorical ambiguity, as being *also* a theory of the living organism, it is particularly illuminating to compare that theory with *Breuer's thinking* as it is articulated at the very same time in the chapter on "Theoretical Considerations" written for the *Studies in Hysteria*. For one would have to limit oneself lazily or thoughtlessly to the most extrinsic formulations in order to consider without discussion what is presented there by Breuer as the initial stage of Freud's thought.[20]

For although their clinical experience is apparently the same—the "retention" of affect in hysterical manifestations and its contrary, "abreaction"—and although the "rule of constancy of sums of excitation" is presented as the first "joint theory" of the two authors (to the point that each attributes it to the other), the divergence between Breuer's physiology in the "Theoretical Considerations" and that which may be derived from the *Project for a Scientific Psychology* is, in fact, profound.[21]

Breuer, it should be recalled, collaborated with Hering in his work on one of the principal self-regulating systems of the organism: breathing. The constancy he refers to is of the same type: a *homeostasis*. Not, of course, a homeostasis of the whole of the organism (like those which regulate the major constants in life), but a homeostasis of a more specific and specialized system: the central nervous system.

It is within that framework that his distinction between a "quiescent" energy or "intracerebral tonic excitation" and a kinetic energy circulating through the system should be understood. The constancy principle, for Breuer, regulates the *base level* of the tonic energy; it is thus unlike the pleasure principle, which, for Freud, will regulate the *flow* of circulating energy.

For this reason Breuer can write: "There exists in the organism a tendency to keep intracerebral excitation constant."[22]

A base level of the kind envisaged is conceived of as an *optimum*. As such, it can be threatened by various changes of level, some effecting a generalized disturbance, others a more localized one; as such, it can be reestablished through a discharge (abreaction) *but also through a recharge*. What is at stake, it may be said, is the maintenance of a veritable energy *Gestalt*.

Finally, that optimum has its own finality: the free and successful circulation of kinetic energy, that is, an uninhibited functioning of thought, the existence of unimpeded associations:

We have spoken of a tendency on the part of the organism to keep tonic cerebral excitation constant. A tendency of this kind is, however, only intelligible if we can see what need it fulfills. We can understand the tendency in warm-blooded animals to keep a constant mean temperature, because our experience has taught us that that temperature is an optimum for the functioning of their organs. . . . I think that we may also assume that there is an optimum for the height of the intracerebral tonic excitation. At that level of tonic excitation the brain is accessible to all external stimuli, the reflexes are facilitated, though only to the extent of normal reflex activity, and the store of ideas is capable of being aroused and open to association in the mutual relation between individual ideas which corresponds to a clear and reasonable state of mind.[23]

Inversely, in dreams, associations will be defective and impeded. In *a thesis diametrically opposed to Freud's*, dreams, for Breuer, manifest a state in which psychical energy is anything but "free," and *that* because of a "decrease" in the base level of tonic potential which is "the very condition of the power of transmissions."[24]

The model used here is one of a network in which modulation is possible only by virtue of a certain electrical base level, which is to be maintained at all costs: the tonic energy has an absolute priority over every possible circulation of the kinetic energy.

This all too brief summary of Breuer's thought should suffice to show the interest merited by a neurophysiological approach which, although starting from the "physicalist" notions of Helmholtz's school, remained extremely flexible and quite close to physiological experience. Such an approach may be considered to be not in rigorous contradiction with later discoveries of neurophysiology (e.g., the maintenance of a base level by the activating reticulated system), and, as such, to be a scientifically plausible and open hypothesis.

Freud, however, in his earliest writings and throughout the length of his work, uses as a fundamental point of conceptual reference the opposition between two types of energy: free energy and bound energy. He attributes the introduction of that distinction in psychology to Breuer and explicitly assimilates his free energy to Breuer's kinetic energy, his bound energy to quiescent energy: "This picture can be brought into relation with Breuer's distinction between quiescent (or bound) and mobile cathectic energy in the elements of the psychical systems."[25]

Reference to the common origins of the theories of Breuer and Freud in Helmholtz's thought should, in principle, allow us better to understand such an assimilation. And, indeed, we do find clearly posited in Helmholtz the distinction between *free energy* and *bound energy*. He introduces these terms in the course of considerations concerning the Carnot-Clausius principle and the degradation of energy. The Carnot principle, as is known, results in the idea that despite the initial definition of energy as "the capacity to produce work" and despite the principle of the conservation of energy, what is conserved in a given system—its total internal energy—is not, for all that, able to be indefinitely reconverted into work. Whence the distinction between two types of energy whose sum constitutes the internal energy: energy that can be reconverted into work and is "usable" (Maxwell), and energy that cannot be reconverted and is "degraded" in the form of heat. It is in order to designate these two types of energy that Helmholtz proposes the terms *free energy* and *bound energy*: "It seems certain to me that we must distinguish, within chemical processes as well, between that portion of the forces of affinity capable of being freely transformed into other kinds of work, and that portion that can only become manifest in the form of heat. To abbreviate, I shall call these two portions of energy: free energy and bound energy."[26] For a given system, this may be translated by the equation:

$$\underset{\text{Internal energy}}{U} = \underset{\text{Free energy}}{F_{(reie)}} \searrow + \underset{\text{Bound energy}}{G_{(ebundene)}} \nearrow = C^{te}$$

In the equation, the free energy (freely usable energy) tends constantly to diminish, whereas the bound (nonreconvertible) energy increases.

Now a certain analogy may be found between this law and that which, in a mechanical system, governs the relative quantities of potential or tonic energy and kinetic energy: like tonic energy, Helmholtz's free energy presupposes a high level of potential and the capacity to be transformed into another form; it resembles tonic energy as well in that it tends to decrease in the course of its different conversions and eventually attains a minimal level, whereas kinetic energy, for its part, can never be completely reconverted into tonic energy.[27] Despite certain details, which are irrelevant in this context, we can propose a second equation, at the level of the mechanical laws governing states of equilibrium:

$$\underset{\text{Total energy}}{E} \; = \; \underset{\text{Tonic energy}}{T} \searrow \; + \; \underset{\text{Kinetic energy}}{C} \nearrow \; = \; C^{te}$$

If, then, a comparison was to be made with the science of physics, it would be between free energy and tonic energy, bound energy and kinetic energy, a comparison which is *exactly* the reverse of the one Freud made in assimilating his own terms, free energy and bound energy, to Breuer's distinction between kinetic energy and quiescent energy.[28]

A misdeal? A double set of cross-purposes? Freud takes up terms charged by Helmholtz with the meaning of the second law of thermodynamics; he more or less reverses their meaning, interpreting the adjective "free" in the sense of "freely mobile" and no longer "freely usable"; finally, he superimposes that opposition on distinctions introduced by Breuer. If, in *The Interpretation of Dreams*, a manifest absurdity corresponds to an ironic criticism to be found in the latent content, we believe ourselves authorized to see in this formally respectful treatment of Breuer's theory the mark of an exasperated irreverence.

And indeed, what a difference between the *reasonable* hypotheses of Breuer and the vast *machinery* of the *Project for a Scientific Psychology*! At the present juncture, that difference may be observed at the very level of the organism. Breuer posits the bases of a viable organism, whose relations with its environment are regulated by homeostases and in which an unimpeded functioning, proper circulation, is second in relation to the maintenance of a proper form. Freud, on the contrary, would deduce within the organism the "secondary function," starting from a primary tendency to evacuate energy. One need only follow carefully the first lines of the *Project*, devoted to the "quantitative line of approach," to see how strange it is.

The principle of neuronic inertia, a principle of absolute evacuation of energy, is from the outset illustrated by what is commonly called *the model of the reflex arc*:[29] the evacuation at the motor end of the excitation received at the receiving end, with the essential postulate that it is the same quantity of the same energy that is carried to one end in order to be restored, in the form of movement, at the other end. It is a naïve model of conduction of received mechanical energy by the nervous system, as if what were under consideration were a hydraulic draining system; it is a model incompatible with physiological discoveries already made by the end of the nineteenth century; a model which Freud himself corrects at times by indicating that what takes place at the motor end is not a simple transmission of energy, but the triggering of a release of internal energy at the level of the "motor neurones";[30] a model which, nevertheless, in its massive mechanistic simplicity, will be rediscovered at the foundation of the evolution of the "living vesicle," as late as in *Beyond the Pleasure Principle*.

Now it is on the basis of this abiological functioning, which seems "deathly" in the very sense of the death drive, that Freud would introduce, through a kind of deductive argument, the constitution of a "reserve of energy." The mediator, in this deduction, is what Freud calls the "exigencies of life," meaning by that the pressure exercised on the organism by a rush of excitation of internal origin, the inadequacy of anarchical organic reactions in durably evacuating that overcharge, and the necessity of triggering appropriate "specific" actions, which are alone able to open the floodgates towards discharge:

The neuronic system is consequently obliged to abandon its original trend towards inertia (that is, towards a reduction of its level of tension to zero). It must learn to tolerate a store of quantity sufficient to meet the demands for specific action. In so far as it does so, however, the same trend still persists in the modified form of a tendency to keep the quantity down, at least, so far as possible and avoid any increase in it (that is, to keep its level of tension constant). All the performances of the neuronic system are to be comprised under the heading either of the primary function or the secondary function imposed by the exigencies of life.[31]

Thus, in the transition from a mechanism regulated only by the death drive to an organization subject to the constancy principle, it is the *very idea of life* that would serve as mediator and catalyst. And on every occasion on which Freud refers to the "biological standpoint" in the *Project for a Scientific Psychology*, he does so in order to bridge the gaping discontinuity in the "mechanistic" argument.

The notion that the *idea* of an organism—the term being taken here with all its connotations, both those of representation and those of *eidos*, "form"—is the factor that "precipitates" the bond and provokes the transition from primary *psychical* functioning to secondary functioning is a conception coherent with the "introduction of the ego" throughout Freud's thought. But the impasse asserts itself when, at the "earlier" level—the deduction of the living and even of "life" itself—it is still the "exigencies of life" that are invoked, as a final cause, in order to justify the constitution of an organism and the maintenance of a store of energy that is "bound" by the very limit of the vesicle: thus we find carried back into the vital order the joint priority or primacy of the reflexive phase and the tendency towards zero, which, nevertheless, finds its justification solely within the field of psychoanalysis.

It remains to *interpret* the triple *Zwang* affirmed in the death drive, to perceive the fundamentally original kind of rationality hiding behind the shocking lack of logic of certain theses: an interpretation, which, in each of its three moments, should attempt to coincide with *a call back to order coming from the unconscious itself.*

The priority of the self-phase? We have shown that whether the subject be autoerotism, fantasy, or masochism, what is being discussed is nothing but the position of the originary character of the reflexive moment for the constitution of human sexuality.

What is being recalled as well is the autonomy of the field of human sexuality as the field of psychoanalysis, the rule according to which there is nothing to be sought "beyond" it in the art of psychoanalytic listening and interpretation, since every unmediated reference to life, self-preservation, and reality falls outside of our grasp.

In addition we find in this thesis the affirmation of fantasy as our primary element, the originary internalization of "conflict" and of the irreconcilable. In this sense, the death drive, a concept that seems quite undialectical, is present, in Freud's final formulations, not as an element in conflict but as *conflict itself* substantialized, an internal principle of strife and disunion.[32]

The priority of zero over constancy? We would see in it the reiterated affirmation of the laws of the unconscious process, in their heterogeneity in relation to everything that depends on the intervention of reality or of the ego. The free circulation of affect, as it is discovered in fantasy or in the laws of dreaming is reasserted: in the *Interpretation of Dreams*, the model of the reflex arc finds its original meaning in a "reflex apparatus," constituted by mnemic or ideational systems. The pleasure principle, radicalized as the Nirvana principle, was discovered and is valid only at the level of ideational representatives, and cannot be merged haphazardly—lest the most utter confusion ensue for psychoanalysis—with apparently similar principles observed within the "vital order."

And yet it is indeed with principles from the vital order that Freud, from the very beginning, would establish a kind of continuity. It is to them that, in *Beyond the Pleasure Principle*, he attributes, as a tendency towards death, a repetition compulsion whose major piece of supporting evidence is, however, the psychoanalytic phenomenon par excellence: transference. We are thus posing the most difficult question when we inquire as to the internal exigency that leads Freud to carry back to the biological level two theses that can be justified only in relation to the discovery of psychoanalysis.

To be sure, the necessity of *affirming the primal or originary*, both in the form of the "individual myth"[33] and in historical or prehistorical myth, may be identified as one of the fundamental, founding orientations of Freud's thought. And asserting the biological myth of the emergence of a living form from a chaos of energy is indeed tantamount to projecting into the same dimension, beyond our grasp, the individual event effecting the coagulation—within what we can imagine only with difficulty under the rubric of the primary process—of the first nucleus of an ego.

And yet if we consider that this carrying back of the present into the past, of ontogeny into phylogeny, is also, in the case at hand, a carrying back of death into life, we are hard put to avoid a more specific interpretation of that movement towards the originary. It is as though there were in Freud the more or less obscure perception of a necessity to refute every vitalistic interpretation, to shatter life in its very foundations, with its consistency, its adaptation, and, in a word, its instinctuality —concerning which we have noted how problematical it is in the case of humans. And in order to do so, to carry death back (and such, of course, is the paradox) to the very level of biology, as an *instinct*. It is not without good reason that the commentators have on more than one occasion noted that at the level of Freud's last "dualism," it is perhaps no longer drives in the "Freudian" sense of the term that are in question, but instincts, in a kind of hyperbolical transcendence of the banal meaning assumed by that term within the life sciences. In order better to understand how this compulsion to demolish life comes to the surface precisely in the year 1919, with the ascendancy of the death drive, several additional considerations concerning the evolution and structure of Freud's theory would be indispensable.

In 1914 "Narcissism: An Introduction," appeared; in 1923, *The Ego and the Id*. This is the period in which, with the development of the theory of the ego and of its narcissistic libidinal cathexis, "life" imposes itself as more pressing and encroaching. The ego now seems to pride itself on all the powers and delegations it has accumulated: the delegations of self-preservation, but also those of sexuality, even including love and object-choice, which are always marked, as we observed, by the stigma of narcissism. Concomitantly, we now observe the emergence of Eros, the divine force that we were not able to examine at any length, but only to emphasize how it differs from sexuality, the first discovery of psychoanalysis. Eros is what seeks to maintain, preserve, and even augment the cohesion and the synthetic tendency of living beings and of psychical life. Whereas, ever since the beginnings of psychoanalysis, sexuality was in its essence hostile to binding—a principle of "un-binding" or unfettering (*Entbindung*) which could be bound only through the intervention of the ego—what appears with Eros is the *bound and binding form* of sexuality, brought to light by the discovery of narcissism. It is that form of sexuality, cathecting its object, attached to a form, which henceforth will sustain the ego and life itself, as well as any specific form of sublimation.

In the face of this triumph of the vital and the homeostatic, it remained for Freud, in keeping with the structural necessity of his discovery, to reaffirm, not only within psychoanalysis, but even within biology (by means of a categorical disregard for epistomological distinctions), a kind of antilife as sexuality, frenetic enjoyment [*jouissance*], the negative, the repetition compulsion. Strategically, the carrying back of the principles of psychoanalysis into the vital order is tantamount to a counterattack, a means of wreaking havoc in the very bases from which one risked being invaded. A subjective strategy? A strategy of the thing itself if it is indeed true that this carrying back into life of an intensely human war was already at the origin of the generalized subversion introduced by sexuality.

The energy of the sexual drive, as is known, was called "libido." Born of a formalistic concern for symmetry, the term "destrudo," once proposed to designate the energy of the death drive, did not survive a single day. For the death drive does not possess its own energy. Its energy is libido. Or, better put, the death drive is the very soul, the constitutive principle, of libidinal circulation.

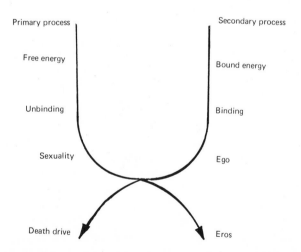

The genealogy of the final instinctual dualism? If we place face to face the terms constituting the constant pairs of opposites in Freud's thought, that genealogy takes the form of a strange chiasmus whose riddle we, as Freud's successors, are beginning to decipher.

Conclusion

As the stages of a meditation on the problematics and history of psychoanalysis, the results presented above have as their principal effect to render more precise the specificity of the field of analysis in relation to the vital order. Now, that specificity is not defined solely through the establishment of an epistemological boundary. It takes on its meaning only if we succeed in elaborating the kinds of relations existing between those two orders: a "genetic" circulation that should allow us to situate the logico-chronological phases of a process of emergence and the modes of transposition from one sphere to the other.

Within human sexuality, the instinct, a vital force, loses its quality and its identity in the drive, its metaphorico-metonymical "derivative." Already the *Three Essays on the Theory of Sexuality*, in their very organization, entailed a radical loss of the biological, even as they posited, in the third chapter ("The Transformations of Puberty"), the scheme through which a different structure could be rediscovered: that resulting from interhuman forms of exchange, a generalized logic of which the oedipal complex is the historically prevalent example.

Within the ego, it is no longer the tension of life but the stable form of the living that is transposed, coming to impose itself by virtue of that primitive physiological weakness that Freud had already designated as the focal point for a specifically human development. The "orthopedic" import of such a form has been emphasized, mainly in order to denounce it, by Jacques Lacan. But considering Freud as the heir of a La Rochefoucauld and a Hegel, analyzing the misprision presupposed by the "reality function" and the defensive or "ideological" alibi lurking behind the ideal of adaptation, is not sufficient to allow one to announce the glad tidings of the "end of the ego," even in the analyst. And this, not only by virtue of the fact that, after all, "life has to be lived" and a human being can supplement a love of life that is occasionally deficient only by a love of the ego or of the ideal agencies which are, in turn, derived from it, but also—if the essence of the ego function is indeed *binding*, before being adaptation—because a minimum of intervention by that function is

125

indispensable for even an unconscious fantasy to *take form*. For fantasy as well as for myth, structuralism has allowed for the elaboration of a combinatorial system, and for showing, after Freud in the *Interpretation of Dreams*, that a symbolic structure should not be confused with the allegedly infinite powers of the imagination [*l'imaginaire*]. And yet even an unconscious fantasy, sustained in the articulation of its terms and in the permutations of its different versions by a fundamental "grammar," could not come into existence without the presence of the minimum of imaginary inertia allowing, along the entire length of the chain, the precipitation of those concretions that are "object-like" in that, like objects, they can be surrounded and cathected: the "ideational representatives."

In order better to grasp what that intervention of the energy of the ego in the sequence of fantasy may be, we may recall, for example, how Freud, throughout his metapsychological texts and as early as 1895, describes the transition of an unconscious idea to the preconscious-conscious level: the verbal representatives are superimposed, through a kind of addition, on the unconscious representative. Properly speaking, this does not entail a conscious sentence duplicating as its translation an unconscious sequence, but rather isolated representatives, individually cathected, inducing locally around each of them an energy field accounting for the phenomenon of "attention." Thus, within the neuronic system of the *Project*, that vast electronic machine initially without boundaries and without an energy of its own, it is the ego, derived from the vital energy form, that introduces the punctuation of recognizable and *reproducible* perceptual elements. It is a punctuation that is perhaps necessary for the fixation of every discursive sequence, even those of the unconscious and, at the other extreme, those of the most highly formalized science.

Opposite the ego, a binding, vital form, the *death drive* is the last theoretical instance serving to designate a logos that would necessarily be mute, were it to be reduced to its extreme state, to the pure predicative movement effecting the flow across the copula of the entire substance of one term into the neighboring term. Which is to say that the conflict between ego and drive, between defense and "wish fantasy," is neither the sole nor the ultimate form of the opposition between *binding* and *unbinding*. At the unconscious level, within the fantasy—at least if it is considered as something other than "pure" free energy—there must indeed be another more fundamental polarity: life drive and death drive, interdiction and desire.[1]

Absent from every unconscious, death is perhaps rediscovered in the unconscious as the most radical—but also most sterile—principle of its logic. But it is life which crystallizes the first objects to which desire attaches itself, before even thought can cling to them.

Appendix:
The Derivation of Psychoanalytic
Entities

The word *derivation* is a term of reference proposed by Michel Foucault in the course of a meditation on the theory of language in the classical age. It serves to designate a problem raised by grammarians like Du Marsais as well as by the *philosophes* of the Enlightenment—a problem concerning the "origins" of language or, more precisely, its very first steps: starting from something in the order of an embryo, those few primitive words that a human animal, still near its "origins," might have possessed. It should be recalled that such a problematic coincides with a hypothesis of Freud, concerning a fundamental "primal language," in relation to which the symbolism we find in dreams and myths would be only a vestige. Starting with these rudimentary words, the eighteenth-century philosophes posed the question of how man may have reached the full richness of our current spoken "natural" languages. These words or primitive roots are alleged to be designations still attached to individual things. They were entirely specific, and the question is, How were they able to be detached from such things? In other words, how did concepts in their universality come to emerge? Foucault summarizes the essential aspect of this process of "derivation" as follows:

In the beginning, everything had a name—a proper or individual name. Then the name became attached to a single element in that thing, and became applied to every other individual which also contained it: it is no longer a specific oak that is called a tree, but everything containing at least a trunk and branches. Names became attached to distinctive circumstances: night designated not the end of the present day, but the slice of darkness separating every sunset from every dawn. Finally, they became attached to analogies: everything that was thin and smooth like the leaf of a tree was called a leaf.[1]

We shall propose three brief remarks concerning this theory and the quoted passage that summarizes its essential aspects. The first is that we have hesitated to specify whether the question in fact bears on the origins of language or on its very first steps. And indeed we are dealing with the first steps, if we consider designations intimately bound to things, simple "signals," as already constituting a first form of "language." But we are dealing with an origin if it is true that the separation between sign and thing, the possibility of the former to circulate independently and be exchanged causes language, properly speaking, to be born.

In the second place, we shall not abandon to others the task of observing that we are here assuming on our own account one of those problems for which our century has in general shown only scorn: a problem of "origins." It is a scorn for wild speculative adventures, as well as for every attempt to inscribe in an empirical, historical genesis a dimension which—since partaking of structure—would constitute the transcendental a priori of every genesis and every history and could consequently not be deduced from them. Isolated in his age, Freud, however, with splendid indifference, seems to continue—at a distance of two centuries—to answer in terms proposed by a provincial Academy for its "competitions": *An Essay on the Origin of Guilt among Men . . . Has Civilization Served to Enrich or Impoverish the Satisfaction of our Instincts?* And it is without the slightest reservation that he accepts the problematic of the origins of language as it is developed in all naïveté in an article by an author named Sperber: "On the Influence of Sexual Factors on the Emergence and the Development of Language."[2] Concerning that article, we shall observe only that its author asserts—exactly like certain philosophes of the eighteenth century—the existence of primitive verbal roots, which (and here is the novelty) would be nothing other than the first cries linked to sexual excitation. With great rapidity, at the very beginning, a bond would be established between those first roots and the first verbalizations linked to work. We are thus faced with a first manner of derivation, in Foucault's sense, a very primitive one, moreover, which leads to a whole series of further ones. In fact these first roots should be conceived of as a kind of nebula, centered above all on action—and consequently on verbs—and from which, through a series of transferences of meaning, nouns, adjectives, and adverbs come to be delimited and stabilized. There is thus a *carrying over* of designation—from the act to its performer, from the act to the way it is performed, etc.—that Sperber attempts to retrace in detail for a few exemplary cases.

In his work on "symbolism," Ernest Jones in turn makes reference to processes of the same type, seeking to assign a common point of origin both to the evolution of mythical, unconscious thought (such as we find at work in psychoanalytic symbolism) and, on the other hand, to precise forms of thought, however purified their concepts may ultimately appear to be.[3]

Finally, and this will be our last preliminary remark, in this entirely hypothetical reconstruction of "origins," we never have at our disposal anything but what is presently observable. The constitutive is reconstructed from the constituted or, in any event, from a constitutive process which is not primal but derived; and that, of course, is the definitive impasse in every quest for origins. Thus, in relation to "the emergence and the development" of a first language, the sliding of designations is inferred only from rhetoric and, more precisely, from that part of it concerned with "tropes": i.e., according to Quintilian, with "felicitous changes of meaning in words or expressions." And it is indeed the path of tropes, even if he does not designate them by their technical names, that Sperber follows in a method invoking current derivations and historical ones (e.g., in the etymology of certain German dialect words derived from High German), in order to sketch an entire series of genealogical trees for the terms under consideration and, from there, to infer by analogy the modalities of pre- or protohistorical derivation he would endeavor to describe.

A critical investigation bearing on a fixed terminological set—that of a certain region of knowledge—cannot fail, the deeper it goes, to pose problems of genesis. Such is the case for a work undertaken with J. B. Pontalis, concerning the "vocabulary of psychoanalysis."[4] Paradoxically, in fact, psychoanalytic terminology is characterized simultaneously by its specificity and by its borrowed or "derived" character. Every psychoanalytic term has an original meaning, linked in a precise way to the body of analytic doctrine. But at the same time, even if some appear to be neologisms, it is not difficult to detect their origin in a number of more or less contiguous regions, among which psychology is far from constituting a privileged source: there are also the sciences of nature, biology, economy, and medicine, to name a few.[5]

Take the example of a term coming from medicine, or more precisely, surgery—"trauma"—which may be discovered at the origins of psychoanalysis, specifically in the inaugural notions of *psychical trauma* and *traumatic hysteria*. *Trauma* is, in fact, an extremely old concept, present at the origins of medicosurgical thought. The trauma, at the beginning, is a wound, conceived of as a "piercing" of the surface of the body. Contemporary theories of physical trauma have completed this first approximation, which identifies trauma and wound and delineates three basic dimensions: (1) a violent shock; (2) a breaking into the organism, entailing the rupture or opening of a protective envelope; (3) finally, the idea of a repercussion on the whole of the organism, resulting in a more or less unadapted, disproportionate and catastrophic global reaction on the part of that organism. Now it is not so simple to retrace the filiation or "transposition" of this notion into psychology and psychiatry. It may be perceived in particular that the notion of a shock with a physical "break-in" and that of a vital danger entailing a general reaction were long maintained at the core of an allegedly psychical symptom—so long, in fact, that in the most recent treatises on surgery, something resembling traumatic neurosis is described as the "subjective syndrome of cranial traumas," and that within a classification under the heading "cranio-cerebral traumas." Such a classification is bound to a theory of psychical trauma which is far from abandoned. There would be a series of gradations linking major impairments of tissue to decreasingly perceptible degrees of damage, but that would nevertheless be of the same nature: histological damage and, ultimately, intracellular damage. The trauma would proceed, as it were, to a kind of self-extenuation, but without losing its nature, until it reached a certain limit, that limit being precisely what we call "psychical trauma."

An entirely different direction was followed first by Charcot, then by Freud. It was Charcot who discovered and named *traumatic hysteria* as a particular category of hysteria which was interesting from a *pathogenic* point of view. As he demonstrated, paralyses of hysterical conversion may also appear following a violent physical shock endangering life. But after the trauma, if one attempts to discover neurological damage or even a correlation with the anatamo-physiology of the nervous system, it becomes clear that they cannot be found: that is what Freud, in an article of the same period directly dependent on Charcot's teaching, formulated with exemplary clarity. Moreover, after the physical trauma, the life-endangering shock, there exists a period of latency, of "incubation" (Charcot) or of "elaboration" (Freud), that would lead one to think of something different from a purely causal physiological sequence. Finally, there is an additional element in Charcot's discovery: the possibility of reproducing experimentally under hypnosis certain hysterical phenomena, in which it is seen that a minimal trauma—an entirely symbolical (and thus entirely "psychical") one—results in effecting at least momentarily a paralysis of the same type. Whence the notion at which Charcot, along with several others, had already arrived, and which Freud (with Breuer) would simply elaborate more successfully: the idea of a "paralysis due to ideas" occurring within a particular psychical state, which either is a precondition, or on the contrary, is provoked by the trauma itself: a veritable stupefaction of psychical defenses known as a "hypnoid state." Thus did the notion of a psychical trauma, through a displacement of the various elements of physical trauma into a different domain, come to be elaborated. It retained the idea of a shock as a brutal rush of excitation and that of a breaking-in as an intrusion into the psyche of a group of ideational representatives that would remain there, a "separate psychical group" or an "alien internal entity." Finally, there is indeed a catastrophic reaction: a disqualification of normal defenses and a triggering of a virtually atopical kind of reaction on the part of the ego, since it begins functioning according to the "primary process" principle which "normally" governs the phenomena of wish and desire and not those of defense. We shall not insist, in the present context, on the originality of this theory of trauma in Freud, which, linked to the notion of *seduction*, ends up going radically beyond the traditional oppositions between the endogenous and the exogenous, the constitutional and the acquired, etc. We prefer to situate ourselves temporarily in an apparently more "formal" perspective, one less bound to the "content" of the concept, in order to note the difference between two modes of derivation: one situating the psychical trauma in a prolongation or a continuation of the medicosurgical theory of the physical trauma; the other transposing more or less analogically the elements of the latter into a different sphere. And, to be sure, we encounter here an opposition between two conceptions, of which one seems, far more than the other, to respect and even to found the specificity of a certain field of knowledge, borrowing from the adjacent field—medical science—only "manners of speaking." We should, all the same, be suspicious of any disqualification of the path of continuity between two adjacent domains: so clear a separation between what is purely somatic and what is purely psychical in the trauma has never been sustained within the Freudian tradition. It should also be recalled what degree of interest was later provoked on the part of Freud and other psychoanalysts by a notion such as Rank's "birth trauma." Who can say whether, at the time of birth, the distinction between physical trauma and psychical trauma is still valid? Who can say whether we do not find there the point of real continuity, "in the beginning," the locus of a kind of internal communication between what will become, respectively, physical trauma and psychical trauma?

It would seem that a concept can be "derived" according to two paths: that of an extension through continuity, an imperceptible transition to an adjacent field; and that of a transposition through similarity into a field that is different but structured as analogous. That observation is quite banal if one considers that continuity and resemblance are the two fundamental types of association posited by every theory of association-ism since the classical era. Continuity and similarity are also the bases of the two principal tropes in rhetoric, if we simplify the deceptive and almost macaronic diversity of figures which rhetoricians have indulged themselves in proliferating. We are indebted above all to Roman Jakobson for this reunification under the twin rubrics of *metaphor* and *metonymy*.[6] In both cases, according to him, there is a transition from a proper, central, primary meaning, independent of the context, to a figurative, marginal, secondary meaning, borrowed from and linked to the context. But what distinguishes metaphor from metonymy is the kind of association between the primary "signified" [signifié] and the secondary "signified": "Metaphor (or metonymy) is the charging of a signifier with a secondary signified associated by resemblance (or contiguity) with the primary signified."[7] Thus metonymy is the trope of contiguity, englobing as one of its subcategories the neighboring trope distinguished by classical rhetoric: synecdoche. For the other trope, metaphor, resemblance constitutes the fundamental link. This second figure is posited by Perelman in his *Traité de l'argumentation*[8] as a similarity of structure or a resemblance of relations establishing a kind of equation of relations: $a/b=c/d$. Thus, in that rather banal metaphor according to which Les Halles are "the belly of Paris," we would have the equation Les Halles /Paris = belly/individual, and the metaphor would be a "condensed analogy resulting from the fusion of an element of the 'phor' [or the relation c/d between terms which underlie the reasoning] with an element of the theme [which is the relation of terms a/b to which the conclusion refers]." The underlying idea, "Paris is an individual," would be what serves to found the possibility of the metaphorical figure.

Without wanting to discuss this example at length, we cannot fail to note that the interpretation of the mechanism it implies is far from univocal. It would be quite arbitrary and hardly plausible to suppose that the assimilation of Paris to an individual constitutes the *actually* or *psychologically* presupposed condition allowing the metaphor to function. It might be claimed, with no less plausibility, that it is the metaphor itself which serves to found the analogical assimilation of the city to an organism. In fact, two paths are opened here, each of which is equally untenable: either reduce the metaphorical movement entirely to the perception of real analogies existing, so to speak, within the "signified"; or consider that the "effects of the signified," which we subsequently observe as analogies, are born solely of the play of "signifiers," of their purely formal algebra. This second interpretation implies that metaphor and metonymy be defined by nothing in the order of reality and perception, but entirely as a function of a *universe of discourse*. It would thus be a matter of two dimensions of language, which are "perpendicular" in relation to each other (if it is indeed true that metonymy calls into play displacements along the axis of utterance, whereas metaphor entails a substitution for any term of one of the innumerable "paradigms" capable of fulfilling an analogous function). We should emphasize that Jakobson, for his part, even if he explicitly relates metaphor and metonymy to these two paradigmatic and syntagmatic dimensions of discourse, never goes so far as to abolish an explicit reference to a prior resemblance or contiguity instituted in the universe of the signified.

Jacques Lacan, as is known, has introduced extensively the distinction between metaphor and metonymy in order to organize in terms of it the phenomena discovered by psychoanalysis. The originality of his position lies, on the one hand, in the ontologically founding value with which he endows these two tropes, and, on the other, in the decision to attribute their efficacy to the "signifying" process *alone*. Thus, in metonymy, it is not an actual contiguity (cause and effect, container and contained, part and whole, etc.) which constitutes the thread along which the slippage is effected, but solely the continuity of the utterance which links the terms together: if "sail" [voile] can be used as a metonymy of "boat" [*bateau*], it is solely as a function of the expression "sailboat" [*bateau à voile*]. The same would hold for metaphor, whose production would totally unrelated to any resemblance or even structural homology between the terms substituted.[9]

Our immediate intention is not to discuss in all its generality the question of the foundation and the ontological function of metaphor and metonymy.[10] If these problems are raised here, it is in regard to a consideration of the quite observable derivations in the particular, though exemplary field constituted by psychoanalysis as a specific discursive domain. We encounter therein, in order to put them to the test in the case of precise examples, a certain number of fundamental questions:

1. Do the processes under consideration have an impact or a resonance within reality or should we restrict them, as the eighteenth century would have, entirely to the process of nomination, to the evolution of vocabulary? In other words, is the genesis we are discussing a sheerly nominal genesis? Is it, to take a step further, a genesis of models? Or, finally, the possible genesis of certain beings, "entities" or "agencies"? And even if we pause temporarily at the middle position, the genesis of models—think, for example, of the biological model so frequently used by Freud—the question nevertheless recurs, What value is to be attributed to a model in Freud's thought? Already, concerning physics, it has been claimed that "the scientists who first described electricity as a current contributed for all time a *form* to that field of science."[11] Even if we admit that for the natural sciences this adherence to a model constitutes a stage which is as yet impregnated with "imaginary" illusions and which formalization should succeed in freeing them from, the question retains its full value for the "human sciences," in which it may be asked whether the model itself does not have a structuring function that is unsurpassable. We should recall here all the importance taken on within Freud's work precisely by the notion of *Vorbild*, translated according to its context as "model" or "prototype," an ambiguity of translation which only reflects the fact that the theoretical "model" is at the same time the first exemplar in a series of real phenomena. Thus, when we admit that sleep is the *Vorbild* of narcissistic states or mourning the *Vorbild* of melancholia, we are dealing with something different from a simple comparison justified by similar mechanisms.

2. We may also pose the question of the reciprocal situation of the derivations we have called metaphorical, on the one hand, and metonymical on the other. Are they opposed to each other? Must we choose

between them? The example of the *trauma* would seem, upon first examination, to constrain us to choose one of the two conceptions: a psychical trauma conceived of as the most refined kind of physical effraction and a psychical trauma analogous to—as though carried over into another sphere—physical trauma. And yet, the analysis of other examples borrowed from psychoanalysis will oblige us perhaps to return to this all too absolute opposition, just as a stylistic analysis does not always allow one to decide in terms of exclusion between uses of each of the two tropes.

3. Finally, insofar as we admit that these are not simply rhetorical figures, but also modes of derivation which perhaps have a value at the level of *psychical being*, can we say that one of the two modes of derivation confers on the *entity* so derived a greater weight than the other? Metaphor is often devalued insofar as it is associated with a mode of thought marked by the "as if" corresponding to the philosophical attitude of pragmatism. "It's only a metaphor" is a remark serving to depreciate the value of the expression referred to. On the contrary, did not metonymical continuity, as it appeared to us in the case of trauma, serve (for those physicians who continued to speak of psychical trauma in the same terms as somatic effraction) to safeguard, in a monistic perspective, the equal measure of reality concealed in both versions of the concept? Is it not in the name of a materialistic monism that the physician persists in alleging the microscopic reality of a trauma which evades his grasp?

A second example, with crucial import for our subject, is furnished by the *Freudian notion of the ego.* As is known, there has been an attempt to oppose two meanings of this term (*Ich*) in Freud: a "nontechnical" sense that would designate as the "ego" the individual, the person in his entirety; and a properly technical and psychoanalytic sense: the ego as an "agency," as evolved in the "second topographical model" alongside the id and the superego. We shall not enter here into the details of the historical problem thus posed by Freud's thought. But the question for us at present is one of knowing what the relation is between these allegedly heterogeneous meanings of a single term: what "derivation" does Freud effect from one to the other? A thorough study of the problem shows that we find the two genealogical lines that we have termed metaphorical and metonymical to be continually present in Freud as well as in his followers.

The metonymical line. The ego is presented as a differentiated organ, the executive agent of the totality it is derived from, and is charged with insuring that the rights of that totality prevail in the face of the contradictory and shattering exigencies of drives, superego, and external reality. The manner in which its genesis is described is familiar: its point of departure (the "perception-consciousness system"), its stratification, its thickening upon contact with reality. There would be a differentiation, of the psyche at its surface, the formation of a perpetually reinforced protective layer that would exercise an increasingly extensive measure of mastery over the deeper layers. Ultimately, in this perspective, the ego is an organ adapted to precise tasks but one which remains in *continuity* with the organism whose specialized appendix it constitutes.

The metaphorical line. This metaphor is *real*; it is an identification. It cannot be forgotten that the ego is an instance or agency *within* the personality and not simply an organ *of* it. To be sure, this agency is constituted in successive phases representing so many deposits or "sedimentations," all of which, however, correspond to imprints or introjections of external images. The first and most fundamental of these images—which is also the most impoverished—is not that of a *particular person*, but of an *other* being in all its abstractness: a *body* apprehended as a totality, defined only by the existence of an envelope separating an "inside" from an "outside." Does not this series of identifications—a primal imprint, then a number of introjections—correspond to the very model of a carrying over into a different sphere: i.e., to the essence of metaphor?

There is perhaps no more surprising passage in Freud than the one in which he has coexisting, without any concern for contradiction, these two geneses and essences of the ego: "The ego is not only a surface, but also the projection of a surface."[12] This enigmatic sentence is commented on in a note in the Standard Edition that received Freud's approbation: "It [the ego] may thus be regarded as a mental projection of the surface of the body [i.e., its psychical metaphor] besides, as we have seen above, being the superficies of the mental apparatus [and there we recognize what we called metonymy]."[13] This ambiguity between metaphor and metonymy may be rediscovered throughout the whole of a text like *Beyond the Pleasure Principle*, in which the model employed, the famous model of the protoplasmic vesicle, moves constantly from one register to the other. We never know whether we are dealing with the biological register proper, i.e., with the image of a living being in its totality, or with the psyche (the "psychical apparatus"), or even with the "ego." Nor can we decide whether each of these registers is considered simply as the image of the other, in a series of successive dovetails, or whether there exists between these images an internal continuity which would be simultaneously temporal, genetic, and spatial.

We believe that any forced choice between these two "conceptions" of the ego would constitute a mutilation of psychoanalytic thought. Any reduction of the ego to a simple function—of "reality" or adaptation, for example—would be tantamount to lapsing to a position prior to all the properly psychoanalytic discoveries, and regressing to what would be the ultimate version of an academic psychology of faculties. But making the ego a "simple" metaphor—i.e., an image whose role in the psychical apparatus would be restricted to delusion and "lure" [*leurre*] (Lacan) —would entail underestimating the effectiveness or sheer weight taken on by that image. Here metaphor as well as metonymy, without the assistance each brings to the other, would bring us to a position that would neglect one of the principal discoveries of psychoanalysis: *the constitution within the subject of veritable internal objects*, or even, to go one step farther, *the constitution of the subject on the model of those objects*. Freud's "anthropomorphism" has been criticized for occasionally resulting in slightly ridiculous formulations, in a "prescientific" realism. In point of fact, such anthropomorphism or psychical realism should be taken literally, as truly constitutive of the human psyche. If we may say that the ego is an actualized metaphor of "totality," as observed through the objects encountered in the first years of existence, it must be conceded that that metaphor is truly impossible to transcend and that there is not a more "scientific" language capable of accounting for it any better. As for the term "actualized," it indicates that we are no longer in the realm of the "verbal" or of the "as if," but in that of the very constitution of psychological being. In our view, the conjunction of the process of derivation through contiguity and of the identificatory process is precisely what assures this "precipitation" of metaphor in reality.[14]

Numerous examples, drawn from the most varied aspects of psychoanalytic conceptualization, could be elaborated, but will simply be evoked here. They show, on the one hand, that the derivation in question goes farther than a simple derivation of notions and that it touches on the scientific status of the realities under consideration, and, on the other hand, that metaphor and metonymy, in varying proportions, are always to some degree present and intersecting.

Such is the case for the twin notions of *the unconscious and the id*. The unconscious was initially described (in the first topographical model) in its narrow relation with repression: it is the place to which the memories of ideational representatives repelled out of consciousness are relegated. It is, in the celebrated phrase, an "*other* scene." And it was indeed that fundamental discovery, which cannot be withdrawn, which allowed us elsewhere to attempt to describe the process of repression on the model of metaphor.[15] But at the same time, and from the very beginning of Freud's thinking, we find as well an entirely different conception of the unconscious which would be *continuous* with the biological level of "needs." In that reversed perspective, consciousness itself would be only the possible —but not necessary—*prolongation* of the unconscious: "Everything that is conscious was initially unconscious." Ultimately, the conception of the *id* simply gives a name to this second point of view, but throughout the entirety of Freud's thought these two conceptions of his principal object coexist: an object that is separated, cut off, *carried over* onto another scene; or, on the contrary, a region of being continuous with the neighboring regions. Freud's spatial diagram of the psychical apparatus in *The Ego and the Id* conveys the necessity of maintaining these two aspects side by side: on the one hand, the id is in continuity with the ego and, at its other extremity, open onto the body; and, on the other, on one side of the diagram, it is radically separated from the ego by the barrier of repression and is constituted by "ideational representatives" of the drive. In turn, the notion of a "representative" of the drive within the psyche is endowed with the dual metaphorical and metonymical meaning implied by every form of delegation.

Can *sexuality*, in the new sense given that term by the discoveries of psychoanalysis, be regarded as having anything at all in common with the prepsychoanalytic or biologistic conceptions of the sexual relation? And yet, in the face of objections that perhaps have in their favor the appearance of logic, Freud firmly insists on his right to designate as sexual oral and anal activities, as well as pleasures. His arguments invoke every possible resource, metaphor (recall the comparison between the sated infant after his need for food has been satisfied and the human being after orgasm) as well as metonymy (the continuity of activities and symptoms, whether the latter be properly genital or sexual in the broad sense).

Nevertheless, the metaphorico-metonymical relation linking sexuality in the psychoanalytic sense and sexuality in the commonplace sense of genitality is not the essential one. A different derivation, a different genesis is revealed to us, in the course of which infantile sexuality frees itself from an entire series of nonsexual activities, emerging, so to speak, from the "propping" [*étayage*] which has it first "leaning" on the self-preservative functions. In the various moments of propping (*Anlehnung*), we constantly rediscover the guiding threads of contiguity and resemblance which cause the drive to emerge from the instinctual function. The two essential phases here are a *metaphorization of the aim*, which brings us from the ingestion of food, at the level of self-preservation, to fantasmatic incorporation and introjection as actual psychical processes, this time at the level of the drive—and, on the other hand, what might be termed, after Jacques Lacan, a *metonymization of the object*, which, substituting for milk what is directly contiguous to it (the breast), introduces that hiatus allowing us to say without contradiction that "finding the object is refinding it," since the rediscovered object is in fact not the lost one, but its metonym.

We shall mention only in passing the case of *symbolism*, for which the analyses of Jones, after those of Freud, allow us to follow, in the case of a precise symbol (e.g., punchinello), the crisscrossing of derivations through resemblance and through contiguity. These are effected as much along actual perceived associative links as along the links of language. It is that crisscrossing alone, that overdetermination of metaphors and metonymies, which endows the symbol with its consistency and psychical effectiveness.

We shall conclude this inquiry with the case of *transference.* "Transference," "metaphor": the word is the same, and it originally means "carrying over." So much so that when "metaphor" came to designate a trope, it was already by metaphor. This is equally the case for the psychoanalytic use of the term *Ubertragung,* and here more than elsewhere the content of the concept and the genesis of the designation are parallel. Which is to say that it was above all in its *metaphorical* dimension—that of *as if,* of misperception, of an error in addressee—that transference was first understood and, as a result, interpreted.

And yet, think of the situation: are we prepared to reduce the working of therapy to the generating of an illusion in order to dissipate it? Is it conceivable that its effectiveness can be reduced to so little? And that even more so nowadays when everyone entering analysis is well aware that he will "have a transference." If a transference takes on the dimensions of an event capable of changing something for someone, it is indeed because, in one of its dimensions, it transcends the fantasmagoria to which it has occasionally been reduced. Is this tantamount to saying that it is in that other dimension that we should be looking for its effectiveness, no longer in the carrying over (of past experiences) into another site, but in the *continuity* of its rhythm with a *vaster form of discourse,* that which we never stop holding with ourselves and which is held with us?

This last remark would open our considerations onto another perspective: the privileged relations existing, on the one hand, between metaphor and space; on the other, between metonymy and time. This juxtaposition is already implied by the use Jakobson makes of the two tropes, since metonymy corresponds for him to the (temporal) dimension of the discursive chain, whereas metaphor consists in a substitution of terms situated at the same level within the space of the code (Saussure's syntagmatic and paradigmatic axes).

Our title tended to suggest that the phenomena of "derivation," described under the rubrics of metaphor and metonymy, might be far more than pure figures of style. Beyond any derivations of vocabulary, beyond even a derivation of new concepts, it is the derivation of certain psychical "beings," the formation of psychical "entities" which we deal with in psychoanalytic practice that may be illuminated through reference to these two fundamental axes.

It would, however, be an undue limitation of our conclusions to restrict them to the formula: the human being is through and through structured by phenomena of language. Would not that be tantamount to forgetting, for example, that at the very level of biology, a phenomenon such as generation may properly be related to these two axes: continuity with the parental organism, resemblance with it. Is not the moment of separation, of birth, the one that introduces the break, making of a simple appendix of the mother a being in her image?

More fundamentally still, at the very level of cellular or chromosomal life, are we not now progressing toward an understanding of processes capable of recreating the "same" out of what was initially in continuity, of moving from unity, within a single molecular structure, to the creation —outside of that structure and through an obscure phenomenon of induction—of a second structure identical to the first? Should the reproduction, the multiplication of the pattern of a "viral" molecule, such as biologists are now beginning to discover, incite us to expand into elementary biology the domains of metaphorico-metonymical derivation?

Yet we in turn should pause, lest we be unduly seduced by the biological metaphor—or fantasy—even if illustrious predecessors, like Freud or Ferenczi, have already shown the way.

Notes

INTRODUCTION

1. See chap. 6.
2. See J. Laplanche, "Interpréter [avec] Freud," *L'Arc*, no. 34 (1968), pp. 37–46.
3. See the Appendix to this volume.
4. See particularly Freud, "The Claims of Psychoanalysis to Scientific Interest," sect. 3: "The Biological Interest of Psychoanalysis," in *The Standard Edition of the Complete Psychological Works of Sigmund Freud*, ed. James Strachey (London: Hogarth Press, 1953–66), 13: 179–82. References to *The Standard Edition* will henceforth be abbreviated as *SE*.
5. E. Jones, *The Life and Work of Sigmund Freud* (New York: Basic Books, 1957), 3: 302–14.
6. "Thoughts for the Times on War and Death," in *SE*, 14: 273–302.
7. Ibid., p. 299.

CHAPTER 1

1. See the Appendix to this volume.
2. "Instincts and Their Vicissitudes," in *SE*, 14: 109–40.
3. *Three Essays on the Theory of Sexuality*, in *SE*, 7: 136.
4. Ibid., pp. 147–48.
5. "Instincts and Their Vicissitudes," p. 122.
6. Ibid., p. 123.
7. Ibid.
8. *Three Essays*, p. 135.
9. Ibid., pp. 182–83. Here, and in other quotations from Freud, the comments in brackets are by J. Laplanche.
10. J. Laplanche and J. B. Pontalis, *Vocabulaire de la psychanalyse* (Paris: P.U.F., 1967). Eng. trans.: *The Language of Psychoanalysis*, trans. D. Michelson-Smith (New York: Norton, 1974).
11. *Three Essays*, p. 181.
12. M. Balint, *Primary Love and Psychoanalytic Technique* (London: The Hogarth Press, 1952), particularly the chapter entitled "Early Developmental States of the Ego: Primary Object Love."
13. *Three Essays*, p. 222.
14. "On Narcissism: An Introduction," in *SE*, 14: 83–84.
15. *Three Essays*, pp. 204–5.

CHAPTER 2

1. J. Lacan was the first to have brought this term into relief. It may be regarded as forming part of Freud's "paraconceptual" apparatus. See the article in Laplanche and Pontalis, *Vocabulaire*, on "Deferred Action" [*Après-coup*].

2. S. Moscovici, *La Psychanalyse, son image, son public* (Paris: P.U.F., 1961).
3. *Three Essays*, p. 133.
4. Ibid., p. 134.
5. Ibid.
6. *An Outline of Psychoanalysis*, in *SE*, 23: 152.
7. "The *Project* was Freud's major effort to force a mass of psychical facts into the framework of a quantitative theory and a demonstration by the absurd that the contents exceeded the framework." P. Ricoeur, *De l'Interprétation* (Paris: Seuil, 1965), pp. 82–83.
8. "I no longer understand the state of mind in which I concocted the psychology; I cannot conceive how I came to inflict it on you. I think you are too polite; it seems to me to have been a kind of aberration." Freud to Fliess, letter no. 36 in *The Origins of Psychoanalysis* (New York: Basic Books, 1954), p. 134.
9. If we admit, along with W. Granoff and F. Perrier ("Le Problème de la perversion et les idéaux féminins," *La Psychanalyse*, no. 7 [1964]), that it is predominantly or even exclusively in the process of *mothering* that what might be called a "perverse relation" in women (analogous to the perversion of fetishism) tends to appear, we thus introduce an argument allowing a reexamination and even an elimination of the "statistical" objection with which Freud countered his own theory of seduction.
10. Freud to Fliess, 21 September 1897, in *The Origins of Psychoanalysis*, p. 216.
11. One need but refer to an article whose title alone is eloquent: "Psychoanalysis and the Establishment of the Facts in Legal Proceedings" (1906), in *SE*, 9: 97–114.
12. On this general subject, see Laplanche and Pontalis, "Fantasme originaire, fantasmes des origines, origine du fantasme," *Les Temps Modernes*, no. 215 (April 1964), pp. 1833–68.
13. See p. 24 and n. 9, chap. 2.
14. See pp. 62–63.
15. *Project for a Scientific Psychology*, in *The Origins of Psychoanalysis*, p. 416.
16. Ibid., p. 406.
17. Ibid., p. 407.
18. Ibid.
19. Ibid.
20. Ibid.
21. Ibid., p. 411.
22. The English translation, "shortly before her puberty," renders the argument totally unintelligible.
23. *Project for a Scientific Psychology*, p. 410.
24. Ibid., p. 413.
25. Freud and Breuer, *Studies in Hysteria*, in *SE*, 2: 6.
26. *The Origins of Psychoanalysis*, p. 416.
27. *Three Essays*, p. 223.
28. S. Ferenczi, "The Confusion of Tongues between Adults and the Child," in *Final Contributions to the Problems and Methods of Psychoanalysis* (London: The Hogarth Press, 1955), pp. 156–57.

CHAPTER 3

1. See the Appendix to this volume.
2. The cortex, the gray matter "lodging" perception and consciousness, is at the *surface* of the brain. But from the embryological standpoint, it is not derived from layers any more "superficial" than is the white matter. And from the standpoint of the anatomophysiological paths, it is the cortex which is farthest from the peripheral receivers. But such is Freud's genius that, in order to describe imaginary structures, he makes use—with exemplary indifference—of an imaginary anatomy.
3. *The Ego and the Id*, in *SE*, 9: 25. Emphasis added.
4. *Seelischer Apparat.* This bizarre compound of words underscores the utter originality of Freud's "realism."

5. *The Origins of Psychoanalysis*, p. 356.

6. "Memory is represented by the differences in the facilitations existing between the neurones." Ibid., p. 361.

7. See pp. 35–38.

8. Chapter entitled "Introduction to the Concept of an 'Ego,' " in *The Origins of Psychoanalysis*, pp. 384–86.

9. Ibid., p. 381.

10. Ibid., p. 385.

11. Ibid., p. 388–89.

12. Ibid., p. 384.

13. Ibid., p. 396. The term "facilitation-compulsion" (*Bahnungszwang*) renders precisely the primary process or free, unbound energy: i.e., the compulsive aspect of unconscious wishes.

14. Ibid., p. 427.

15. Ibid., p. 384.

16. Ibid., p. 390.

17. Ibid., p. 393.

18. Ibid., p. 395.

CHAPTER 4

1. During "seventeen delicious days" spent in Rome with Minna Bernays. See Jones, *Freud*, 2: 109.

2. "Tomorrow I am sending you the 'Narcissism,' which was a difficult birth and bears all the marks of it." Freud to K. Abraham, 16 March 1914, in *A Psychoanalytic Dialogue: The Letters of Sigmund Freud and Karl Abraham, 1907–1926* (New York: Basic Books, 1965), p. 167.

3. Section on "Apparent Approach to Jung's Views," in "The Libido Theory" (1923), in *SE*, 18: 257. Freud suggests that his narcissistic phase was a temptation by the energy-monism of Jung and consequently a moment of closure.

4. Ovid, *Metamorphoses* 3. 339–510.

5. Ibid., 446–54.

6. Ellis had mentioned much more than P. Näcke, to whom Freud refers but who did little more than coin the term "narcissism." We touch here on Freud's ambiguous relations with Havelock Ellis, however favorable Ellis may have been to the clinical findings of psychoanalysis.

7. "On Narcissism," p. 88.

8. Ibid., p. 75.

9. Ibid.

10. Translator's note: "Investment" (Fr. *investissement*) is a literal rendering of Freud's *Besetzung*, normally translated as "cathexis."

11. "Formulations on the Two Principles of Mental Functioning," in *SE*, 12: 220.

12. "On Narcissism," p. 76.

13. Ibid., p. 77. Emphasis added.

14. Ibid., p. 76.

15. "The Libido Theory," p. 257.

16. An elaborate note in the *Standard Edition* (19: 63–66) summarizes these fluctuations.

17. On this question, see the article on "anaclitic" in Laplanche and Pontalis, *Vocabulaire*.

18. "On Narcissism," p. 87. This reference to the old notion of an experience of satisfaction (from the *Project* and *The Interpretation of Dreams*) serves to confirm that that notion, as well as that of the "propping" of the sexual drives on the instincts of self-preservation, function in precisely the same domain.

19. Ibid.

20. Ibid., p. 90.

21. Ibid., p. 88.

22. See the Appendix to this volume.

23. "On Narcissism," p. 88.

24. I have sketched out elsewhere these symmetrical movements in object-choice concerning the loves of Hölderlin's Hyperion: *Hölderlin et la question du père* (Paris: P.U.F., 1961), chap. 2, "Les Dialectiques de l'Hypérion."

25. "On Narcissism," p. 90.

26. Ibid., p. 91.

27. Melanie Klein describes infantile megalomania as a defense mechanism occurring at specific moments and not as the initial stage of psychical development.

28. But resembling in inspiration such Freudian distinctions as the source, impetus, aim, and object of the drive.

29. A unique trait which Lacan, properly insisting on its "signifying" aspect, has called the *trait unaire*.

30. "Negation," in *SE*, 19: 237.

31. J. Lacan, "Le Stade du miroir comme formateur de la fonction du Je telle qu'elle nous est révélée dans l'expérience psychanalytique," *Revue française de psychanalyse* 13 (1949): 4.

32. *The Ego and the Id*, p. 26.

33. Ibid.

34. *The Origins of Psychoanalysis*, pp. 381-82.

35. Ibid., p. 381.

36. Anxiety, in relation to the limits of the ego, is the precise metaphor of pain in its relation to the limits of the body.

37. And not between the sexual drives and the ego-instincts or the instincts of self-preservation, as Freud believed on certain occasions.

CHAPTER 5

1. Except as an object of criticism when Adler proposes it.

2. *New Introductory Lectures on Psychoanalysis*, in *SE*, 22: 104.

3. Our usage here differs from that of Melanie Klein, for whom "sadism" is purely and simply a synonym of aggressiveness or destructiveness. With her too there is a slippage of meaning, but the movement is from the sexual sense to the nonsexual sense, and in addition, there is no retention of that first meaning nor of the transition itself. There has simply been a change of meaning, a desexualization of sadism.

4. *SE*, 14: 128.

5. "Instincts and Their Vicissitudes," p. 128.

6. Ibid.

7. The connection established by Freud between the instinctual—or better, drive—"vicissitudes" (*Triebschicksale*), on the one hand, and grammatical transformations, on the other, while remarkably innovative and intriguing is somewhat clouded by a certain confusion. Thus Freud confuses the "middle" and "reflexive" voices. And yet there is every reason to distinguish the middle from the reflexive form within the structure of fantasy, just as they are quite distinct grammatically and semantically, even if the *form of their expression* is occasionally identical. Thus the expression *se cogner* ("to knock [oneself]") corresponds both to the middle form (*En marchant dans l'obscurité, je me suis cogné à la table*, "Walking in the dark, I knocked [myself] into the table") and to the reflexive form (*Je me cogne la tête contre les murs*, "I knock [myself] my head against the walls"). The reflexive form distinguishes more clearly the subject and the object of the action, allowing the fantasied exchanges of position to take place. In the "middle" form, the terms of the fantasy remain in something of a state of coalescence.

8. "Instincts and Their Vicissitudes," p. 130.

9. "The Economic Problem of Masochism," in *SE*, 19: 163.

10. Ibid., p. 164.

11. Ibid. Emphasis added.

12. "Instincts and Their Vicissitudes," p. 130.

13. There is an absolute realism of the thought process; thought is in the body, in the head, and is an internal object—which is to say that in a certain sense, there is no "scientific psychology" based on psychoanalysis.

14. "The dream *is* the fulfillment of a wish"; "the hallucination *is* a satisfaction"—these theses, which are central to psychoanalysis, defy every experimental observation. Freud, moreover, has a certain difficulty in fending off the objection that would admit that dreams express intentions and meanings, but would refuse the notions that those meanings are solely wishes or desires. For indeed, why not include as well hope, fear, resignation, regret, etc.? In order to justify Freud's a priori position (beyond any verification, which would always be suspect), we would have to admit that the fantasy *is in itself* a sexual perturbation.

15. We speak here of a "first pain" as Freud, in the *Project*, speaks of a "first hysterical lie or deceit." The two models are connected in an essential way.

16. "A Child Is Being Beaten," in *SE*, 17: 186.

17. See p. 93.

18. *SE*, 12: 185.

19. Ibid.

20. Ibid., p. 199.

21. Ibid., p. 187.

22. Ibid., p. 190.

23. Ibid., p. 187.

24. We are not, of course, suggesting that this triangle of rivalry is chronologically "prior" to the "sexual" triangle of the oedipus complex.

25. Where shall we situate the third stage of the fantasy "A child is being beaten"? Freud himself hesitated to qualify it as either sadistic or masochistic and finally concluded that "only the *form* of this fantasy is sadistic; the satisfaction which is derived from it is masochistic." *SE*, 17: 191.

The question strikes us as somewhat formalistic to the extent that we, along with Freud, would affirm "the regular and close connections of masochism with its counterpart in instinctual life, sadism." "The Economic Problem of Masochism," p. 163. That complementarity, authorizing us to retain the concept of "sadomasochism," has nothing to do, it should be emphasized, with an actual complementarity between the sadistic and masochistic *perversions*, nor with the possibility of an actual transition from one to the other (through a "turning round," for example). Perversion always presupposes the fixation of *ego* at one of the poles of the fantasy. The diagram we have extracted from "Instincts and Their Vicissitudes" shows in its simplicity that there can be no direct transition from position *S* to position *M*, even though they both stem from a common "primal fantasy."

But in that case, the conscious fantasy "a child is being beaten" should be considered neither sadistic nor masochistic *in the sense of a perversion*. As a sadomasochistic fantasy, it is part of "reflexive masochism," which can also be considered as "reflexive sadism." In "Instincts and Their Vicissitudes" Freud treats "reflexive" masochism as a characteristic of obsessional *neurosis*, and it is not by chance that the patients Freud refers to in "A Child Is Being Beaten" present symptoms which are predominantly obsessional. Thus "Ein Kind wird geschlagen = a child is being beaten" is a neutralized, neurotic, conscious derivative of the primal reflexive fantasy.

CHAPTER 6

1. This ambiguity of the concept of pleasure cannot be entirely eliminated through a terminological convention. It is the index of a process of metaphorization.

2. *Three Essays*, p. 201.

3. In view of the development of physics, we have no reason, in fact, to imagine that "brute" matter necessarily represents the least organized state of matter, and even less to think that it corresponds to the leveling of energy—all differences of potential reduced or abolished—which Freud would suggest.

4. D. Lagache, "Situation de l'agressivité," *Bulletin de Psychologie*, 1961, pp. 99–112.

5. See Laplanche, "Interpréter [avec] Freud," *L'Arc*, no. 34 (1968), pp. 37–46.

6. *An Outline of Psychoanalysis*, p. 192.

7. *Beyond the Pleasure Principle*, in *SE*, 18: 48. The discussion of biological experiments on the survival of unicellular organisms in a suitably nourishing milieu resulted in the conclusion that the organisms would perish only if the milieu was not periodically purged of the toxins produced by cellular metabolism. Freud sees in this proof that "an infusorian . . . if it is left to itself, dies a natural death owing to its incomplete voidance of the products of its own metabolism" (p. 48). Thus the cell dies for "internal" reasons provided that we leave it in the midst of its wastes—that is, provided that we enlarge the organism so that it includes its surroundings. In this kind of argument we recognize the metaphorical pendant of the internalization—in trauma—of the "irreconcilable" drive and of the element of strife that it conveys.

8. *Civilization and Its Discontents* (1930), in *SE*, 21: 119.

9. "Psychoanalysis" (1026), in *SE*, 20: 265.

10. "In the unconscious, however, there is nothing to give content to our conception of the destruction of life. . . . I therefore maintain that the fear of death is to be regarded as an analogue of the fear of castration." *Inhibition, Symptom, and Anxiety*, in *SE*, 20: 146.

11. "The Claims of Psychoanalysis to Scientific Interest," p. 179.

12. Jones, *Freud*, 3: 279.

13. On this subject we have had occasion to refer to Melanie Klein, but we may also invoke Balint, and Bowlby as well in an article which, once reinterpreted, proves extremely useful: "The Nature of the Infant's Relation with His Mother," *International Journal of Psychoanalysis* 39, pt. 5 (1958).

14. "The Economic Problem of Masochism," p. 163.

15. A number of the characteristics of Freud's pleasure principle are already present in the text published by Fechner in 1848: "Uber das Lustprinzip des Handelns," in *Zeitschrift fur Philosophie und Philosophische Kritik* (Halle, 1848). What we encounter in Fechner is by no means a traditional hedonism: the representation of *future* pleasure or unpleasure is irrelevant. The pleasure principle is a regulating mechanism requiring a *present* sensation to bring everything into action. It functions at the level of the pleasure-unpleasure linked to the ideational representatives themselves, and not to what is represented, aimed at, or projected. Since the movement is always from unpleasure toward pleasure, it will be appreciated that within that pair the motivating term is unpleasure. Freud, as is known, began by speaking of an "unpleasure principle," then of an "unpleasure-pleasure" principle; he asserts on several occasions that there is an *automatic regulation* of psychical processes by this principle; ultimately he situates the principle as regulating the "course of ideational representatives." In each of these moves he is adopting Fechner's theses.

16. *Beyond the Pleasure Principle*, pp. 8–10.

17. Ibid., p. 9.

18. It will be useful at this point to transcribe the passage from Fechner quoted by Freud in *Beyond the Pleasure Principle*: "In so far as conscious impulses always have some relation to pleasure or unpleasure, pleasure and unpleasure too can be regarded as having a psycho-physical relation to conditions of stability and instability. This provides a basis for a hypothesis into which I propose to enter into greater detail elsewhere. According to this hypothesis, every psycho-physical motion rising above the threshold of consciousness is attended by pleasure in proportion as, beyond a certain limit, it approximates to complete stability, and is attended by unpleasure in proportion as, beyond a certain limit, it deviates from complete stability; while between the two limits, which may be described as qualitative thresholds of pleasure and unpleasure, there is a certain margin of aesthetic indifference." Fechner, *Einige Ideen zur Schöpfungs- und Entwicklungsgeschichte der Organismen* (1873) pt. 11, Supplement, p. 94.

Freud cannot have failed to perceive the rigorous solution Fechner contributed to the problem of zero and constancy. And yet two lines after this quotation, Freud again offers one of those deliberately vague formulations in which the maintenance of constancy figures as no more than an imperfect approximation of the tendency toward the lowest level.

19. *The Origins of Psychoanalysis*, p. 373.

20. That, however, is precisely what S. Bernfeld does in an article whose sole merit lies in its being one of the first to devote any attention to Breuer's thought; see "Freud's Earliest Theories and the School of Helmholtz," *The Psychoanalytic Quarterly* 13, no. 3 (1944).

21. We can find vestiges of that divergence even in the vicissitudes of the "constancy principle" in the different stages of composition of the only chapter of the *Studies on Hysteria* signed by both authors, the "Preliminary Communication" of 1893.

In a letter to Josef Breuer dated 29 June 1892 (*Gesammelte Werke*, 17: 5), Freud first refers—as if to a commonly held theory—to the "theorem of the constancy of the sum of excitation," but without specifying its contents. In a preparatory manuscript composed together, the principle is said to be a principle of *constancy*, the discharge being only the *means* of reestablishing that "condition of health." *Gesammelte Werke*, 18: 12–13. In the text published by both authors and subsequently inserted into the *Studies on Hysteria*, the "Preliminary Communication" of 1893, *every reference to the principle has been eliminated.* Now, at the same time that the "Preliminary Communication" was being published, Freud delivered a lecture on the same subject to the Vienna Medical Society, a presentation of which a summary has been published, and which "bears all the marks of being the work of Freud alone." Strachey, preface, *SE*, 3: 26. There the principle reappears in a form which no longer alludes to constancy but only to a necessary *discharge*: "If a person experiences a psychical impression, something in his nervous system which we will for the moment call the sum of excitation is increased. Now in every individual there exists a tendency to diminish this sum of excitation once more, in order to preserve his health." Lecture, "The Psychical Mechanism of Hysterical Phenomena," *SE*, 3: 36. Thus it would seem that after working together on a formulation moving in the direction of a *principle of constancy*, Freud and Breuer diverged (explicitly or not), with the result that the point was excluded from publication. Thereupon Freud exploited his new freedom by formulating in more clinical terms a principle of discharge closely related to the *principle of inertia* or the zero principle.

22. *Studies on Hysteria*, p. 197.

23. Ibid., p. 198.

24. Ibid., p. 195.

25. *Beyond the Pleasure Principle*, p. 26.

26. H. Helmholtz, "Uber die Thermodynamik chemischer Vorgänge" (1882), in *Abhandlungen zur Thermodynamik chemischer Vorgänge* (Leipzig: Engelman, 1902), p. 18.

27. "A system is in a state of stable equilibrium when its potential energy possesses one of its minimal possible values." D. O. Chwolson, *Traité de Physique* (Paris: Hermann, 1906), p. 117.

28. This set of cross-purposes has been observed by L. B. Penrose, "Freud's Theory of Instinct," *International Journal of Psychoanalysis*, vol. 12, p. 92: "It should be noted in passing that throughout his analyses Freud seems to depend on a terminology opposed to the one in common use: he calls potential energy *free energy* and kinetic energy—which we call free energy—*bound energy.*"

29. *The Origins of Psychoanalysis*, p. 357.

30. Ibid., pp. 383–84.

31. Ibid., p. 358.

32. "Analysis Terminable and Interminable," in *SE*, 23: 246.

33. See Lacan, "Le Mythe individuel du névrosé ou 'poésie et vérité' dans la névrose" (Lecture at the Collège Philosophique). In a similar way, Freud had already spoken of the neurotic's "family romance." *SE*, 9: 235–41.

CONCLUSION

1. See J. Laplanche, "La Défense et l'interdit dans la cure et la conception psychanalytique de l'homme," *La Nef*, no. 31 (July–October 1967), pp. 43–55.

APPENDIX

1. *Les Mots et les choses* (Paris: Gallimard, 1966), p. 129.

2. H. Sperber, "Uber den Einfluss sexueller Momente auf Entstehung und Entwicklung der Sprache," *Imago* 1, no. 5 (1912): 405–53.

3. E. Jones. "The Theory of Symbolism," in *Papers on Psychoanalysis* (London: Bailliere, 1948).

4. Laplanche and Pontalis, *Vocabulaire de la psychanalyse*, trans. Michelson-Smith, as *The Language of Psychoanalysis*.

5. On this subject see D. Anzieu, "Réflexions sur le Vocabulaire de la Psychanalyse," *Bulletin de Psychologie* 10 (1967): 126–32.

6. R. Jakobson, with M. Halle, *Fundamentals of Language* (Paris: La Harpe, 1956).

7. R. Jakobson, "A la recherche de l'essence du langage," in *Problèmes du langage*, coll. "Diogène" (Paris: Gallimard, 1966), p. 34.

8. C. Perelman, *Traité de l'argumentation* (Paris: P.U.F., 1958), 2: 534–42.

9. J. Lacan, "L'Instance de la lettre dans l'inconscient ou la raison depuis Freud," in *Ecrits* (Paris: Seuil, 1966). Translation in *Structuralism*, ed. J. Ehrmann (New York: Anchor, 1970). Such an orientation has the effect of blurring somewhat the distinction between metaphor and metonymy. For since every reference to the "signified" is rejected, the category of trope is defined entirely by the relation—*within the language structure*—joining the signifiers which are brought into play. But whether that relation be one of continuity within a discursive sequence or be reduced to the "vertical dependencies" of a signifier, in both cases what is under consideration is membership in a given set, and consequently, in the final analysis, *contiguity*. As a result, if we bracket the signified, Lacan's examples do not always allow us to decide whether we are dealing with metaphors or metonymies. If metaphor is defined solely by the formula "one word for another," or simply as substitution, *sail* [*voile*] for *boat* [*bateau*] should correspond to the same mechanism. And if metonymy is based only on the word-by-word connections produced by discourse, might not every metaphor find at least a potential basis in a proposition that links its terms?

In point of fact, one has the impression that for Lacan there is an implicit primacy granted to metonymy, which is less corrupted by empirical elements, and that metaphor, despite all his efforts, remains marked by that perception of resemblances in which Lacan detects the sign of the "imaginary." Despite his asserted intentions, Lacan at times seems unable to avoid devaluing metaphor, as though maintaining it at a distance from being: "If the symptom is a metaphor, it is no metaphor to say so, nor to say that man's desire (or wish) is a metonymy. For the symptom *is* a metaphor, whether or not one is prepared to admit it, just as desire *is* a metonymy, even if men chaff at it." "L'Instance de la lettre," pp. 80–81. Here metaphor, *mere* metaphor, is opposed (as the verbal? as the purely subjective?), at least at the secondary level of scientific elaboration, to an utterance alleged to pronounce a truth beyond the figures of language.

10. We should emphasize that we reject the idea of an absolute primacy of the "signifier." Metaphor and metonymy may be conceived of only as dialectical movements which find their mainspring in the play of signifiers, but which always depend on pre- or paralinguistic contiguities or resemblances and end up restructuring and enlarging the universe of the "signified." Metaphor and metonymy are ultimately marked by the contiguities and resemblances of the *vital order* against which they emerge.

11. Swann Harding, *Philosophy at the Tower of Babel*, quoted by Perelman, *Traité de l'argumentation*, 2: 517.

12. *The Ego and the Id*, p. 26.

13. Ibid.

14. The ego is an object, an internal reality, the metaphor of the individual. As an object, it is cathected by drives and is a reservoir or accumulator of "sublimated libido." It is that economic status which allows the ego to be a center of action, taking over on its own account and energizing functions which, biologically speaking, belong not to the ego, but which are prior to it and continuous with the biological individual: motility, perception, and, more generally, the sphere of "self-preservation."

15. J. Laplanche and S. Leclaire, "L'Inconscient: Une étude psychanalytique," *Les Temps modernes*, no. 183 (July 1961), pp. 81–129. English translation by P. Coleman in *French Freud: Structural Studies in Psychoanalysis*, Yale French Studies 48 (New Haven, 1973).

Index of Freudian Terms